Makerspaces
Top Trailblazing Projects

ALA TechSource purchases fund advocacy, awareness, and accreditation programs for library professionals worldwide.

Makerspaces
Top Trailblazing
Projects

A LITA Guide

Caitlin A. Bagley

An imprint of the American Library Association

CHICAGO   2014

Caitlin A. Bagley is an instruction librarian at Gonzaga University in Spokane. Her research has focused on shifting library technologies and most recently on using infographics in instruction. She has authored several articles on cloud computing and infographics. She is a 2013 ACRL Immersion Teaching with Technology graduate. Bagley earned her master's degree in library science at Indiana University.

Printed in the United States of America

18 17 16 15 14   5 4 3 2 1

Extensive effort has gone into ensuring the reliability of the information in this book; however, the publisher makes no warranty, express or implied, with respect to the material contained herein.

ISBNs: 978-1-55570-990-7 (paper); 978-1-55570-991-4 (PDF); 978-1-55570-992-1 (ePub); 978-1-55570-993-8 (Kindle). For more information on digital formats, visit the ALA Store at alastore.ala.org and select eEditions.

Library of Congress Control Number: 2013050266

Book design in Berkeley and Avenir. Cover images © Shutterstock, Inc.

♾ This paper meets the requirements of ANSI/NISO Z39.48-1992 (Permanence of Paper).

Contents

Introduction

Makers in the Library:
Fostering Creativity and Invention

The culture of makerspaces is all around us; it just takes some careful observance to see them. Chances are high that you are a maker yourself. Have you ever knitted, crocheted, or painted? Have you ever assembled your own home computer or modified your bike or car to go faster? Being a maker or working in a makerspace does not require you to have a high-level skill set. Rather, it teaches you new skills. In one sense, it is enlightening because no one need feel intimidated when going to a makerspace. There you will find you are not alone. Even better, you may know more than you thought you did.

When I first set out to document makerspaces across the nation, I struggled with how to define a makerspace and where exactly they could be found. As a nascent technology in libraries, they were far and few between, though as I began to research I found more and more springing up in new places. My methodology involved designing a survey that would address the physical, technological, and monetary needs, as well as the demographics of the patrons using the makerspaces that were either currently in use or in the process of being developed. I promoted the qualitative survey—composed of twenty-four questions in three major sections—on library listservs and ALA TechSource's social media channels.

As the movement was still quite young, I knew it would be hard to find enough fully operational makerspaces to describe a meaningful variety of projects. I chose to include makerspaces that were in the planning process and would be opening up in 2014, describing design and technical decisions still in process. Respondents were either self-identified as having a makerspace or recruited based on publicity about their project.

This book is best used as not a prescriptive guideline for all who wish to create a makerspace in their own libraries, but as a place to quickly gather information on what others are doing—while also leaving room for your own individual ideas and creativities.

As digital content proliferates, the purpose of libraries is often called into question. Almost any librarian could easily defend libraries' value in innumerable ways, but after one has finished with the defense, another important question remains: what are the key roles and tasks we should be doing to sustain our libraries?

■ ■ ■

Makerspaces operate in an almost ephemeral world. There is not a true uniform definition of what a makerspace can be, which can be both a blessing and a curse when it comes to identifying one. As you read through this book you will find all sorts of makerspaces, each doing something unique and different, all under the makerspace moniker. They live in public libraries, academic libraries, and even school libraries.

Not unsurprisingly, very little has been published on the subject of library makerspaces in general or their pedagogical backgrounds in particular. Much of the literature drawn on pedagogy was taken from similarly based projects in learning centers or communal learning environments. One common theme I found among library learning centers and media centers using new modes of teaching with technology was that learners require the space to discover and learn on their own—and as they do this, they gain a higher degree of self-satisfaction (Carmichael 2009). The act of independent creation encourages return visits. The motivation for offering a makerspace is to encourage a love of learning. In order to do so successfully, the makerspace provider must first identify a learning style or mode to promote. For example, with hands-on learning and modeling, people use a kinesthetic learning style. This is not a reliance on superior motor ability, but rather a focus on learning at one's own speed by one's own hands. Additionally, makerspaces encourage collaborative learning that has a focus on interpersonal and small group skills as well as creating a sense of accountability (I-Sha, Tiong, and Seng 2008). Naturally, different makerspaces will focus on different learning styles. A school or public makerspace that is focused on children may have a stronger emphasis on kinesthetic learning than a makerspace focused on adults, which might lend itself more to group learning. Facilitating group learning—whether through an information commons or a makerspace—is usually a core tenant of academia. Attracting more patrons to work collaboratively is consistent with the mission statements of most libraries.

Makerspaces are certainly unique and original, but the most important question librarians ask is: how are they relevant to libraries? Good question. Libraries are standing on a weird precipice right now. Our patrons need more help than ever using technology and interpreting a sometimes overwhelming glut of information; at the same time, they often view us as being bound to the old model of print. Not to knock print, but any practicing librarian knows that it is just one part of what libraries are about today. Libraries are community centers, and we should think of makerspaces as places for our communities to gather and learn how to create and build together as a community.

Inside these pages you will find examples of libraries that have taken varied approaches to makerspaces with a wide range of budgets and project offerings, as well as a few general practices that should be applicable to most libraries. They have done so. Find what intrigues you, and take a few ideas and run with them.

■ ■ ■

I would like to extend my gratitude to the libraries and librarians who helped me to bring this book to fruition. In particular I would like to thank: Anchorage Public Library, Brooklyn Public Library, Carnegie Public Library, Cleveland Public Library, Georgia Tech Libraries, Mesa Public Library, the Michigan Makers Group, Urbana Free Library, and Valdosta State University Libraries. In addition to these libraries, many of their staff members were willing to correspond with me. They graciously answered my survey and my many follow up emails. They include: Paul B. Baker, Melissa Morrone, Corey Wittig, C. J. Lynce, Charlie Bennett, Sarah Prosory, Ellen Gustafson, Joel Spencer, and Michael O. Holt.

REFERENCES

Carmichael, Patricia. 2009. "The Pedagogy of the Heart and the Mind-Cultivating Curiosity and a Love of Learning, Part 1." *School Library Media Activities Monthly* 25, no. 5: 55–58.

I-Sha, Isabel, Douglas Lau Chin Tiong, and Hilary Ho Oon Seng. 2008. "Designing a Collaborative Learning Space Using Pedagogical Principles: The National Institute of Education's LearningHub@LIBRIS Revisited." *Singapore Journal of Library & Information Management* 37, no. 7: 35–47.

About Makerspaces
Concerns and Considerations

As I discussed makerspaces with people who were not familiar with them, it quickly became apparent that the same questions come up again and again. The following chapter aims to address concerns that may not be mentioned in other places within the book; it also speaks to more general matters common to library makerspaces. Consider this a general FAQ section of the book, shedding some light on basic questions such as "What is a makerspace?" "Why do I need one in my library?" and "What if my library can't afford one?"

DEFINING THE MAKERSPACE

As mentioned in the introduction, this book uses the term *makerspace* to refer specifically to a space that has been designed to allow users to create, build, and learn new projects and technologies.

People often ask how a makerspace differs from a hackerspace. Hackerspaces have been around for slightly longer than makerspaces and exist as a sort of older sibling. Hackerspaces tend to be designed around a group of people coding and creating of software together. Events at hackerspaces can vary depending on how many projects groups are working on and what the focus of the event is. Generally speaking, though, they are set as places for groups to come together to work and learn, pooling their mental resources.

Makerspaces revolve around people creating and working together to build unique items, using a supply of tools would be inaccessible or expensive for individual users. While makerspaces use some elements common to hackerspaces, the makerspace focuses more on creating something tangible that can be taken away from the space. Most libraries are choosing to focus on makerspaces instead because these offer more options for a wider variety of learning styles, skills, and projects.

JUSTIFYING A MAKERSPACE FOR YOUR LIBRARY

As you read this book, you may wonder if makerspaces are really needed in the library environment. Certainly they are not unique to the libraries, as they can be found in a number of different environments—and frequently they exist as their own solo project, unassisted by another institution. Libraries definitely operate on restricted budgets, and they do not necessarily need new library events and spaces to draw away from other programming. So why would anyone want to jump on the makerspace bandwagon and start their own?

First, libraries exist to bring opportunities to their patrons and to promote learning. A makerspace does not require an all-encompassing space, nor will it take over the entire library. It can be as small as a corner or nook—space enough for your patrons to get hands-on learning that they would not otherwise have available to them.

Some makerspaces have generated an aura that makes some librarians uncomfortable. Part of this is a wariness of getting caught up with the "flavor of the moment" and being afraid that the library will make a large financial commitment to something that will not last beyond a few years. Listen to your patron community and see what they want. They might not yet have the words to specifically say that they want a makerspace, but perhaps they want a space where they can work on hobbies and construction projects away from the house. Maybe they're eager to understand how AutoCAD works, but they're confused about the first steps. Maybe they have been telling you about a great prototype for an iPhone application they've come up with but have no way to finance the production of, or a homeowner who wants to build a scale model of a home renovation they're planning. These are all people who are in need of the services of a makerspace, but who may not be aware that these are things the library could offer them for free or at reduced cost. If your library is using the "it's just a trend" argument to hold off on implementing a makerspace, consider the following reasons for why it might be time to get over your fears and start building one.

Few makerspaces actually require intense new construction or renovation of old spaces. They just require equipment, programming, and a place for the equipment to be stored when not in use, as well as room for groups to work together. Does your library have a meeting room that patrons can reserve to study or work on large independent projects? Why not take advantage of the space on days when it is not in use? Some libraries have dedicated days where their meeting rooms are closed off for workshops, and this model can be applied to makerspaces. Other examples are young adult and children's areas, which often have more room to explore and work on projects than the rest of the library. If the focus of your makerspace is aimed at particular populations such as young adult services or children, it may be possible to merge makerspace technologies with areas that have already been developed for these groups. Most of these spaces will already have computers, worktables, and open space for project construction. If the events are held only once or twice a week, it will not be a major upset to the environment to add these elements to the areas for a few hours of the week. Consider bringing in tables and workstations for patrons to use in the space. Most libraries have a few extra tables that do not get used regularly; it may be possible to move these tables to the makerspace location while activities are taking place and then to move them back to their previous locations during downtime, being sure to remain aware of fire code as you move furniture about. This will involve some small amount of prep on staff's part, but it is not an overwhelming project for most libraries to take on. Some libraries even have all their makerspace equipment on one cart that they can roll in and out of storage as needed.

Although makerspace materials can be expensive to purchase, supplying them to your patrons greatly reduces the cost for those who would likely never be able to purchase these materials on their own. This is particularly the case for one-time projects where the cost of expensive machinery cannot be justified for the average person. Some classic analogs to this are videos and DVDs, videogames, and cameras. These devices and items are not books—and they are smaller and generally cheaper than some other makerspace items—but what they do have in common is that they involve technologies not usually associated with a library. This is our time to embrace the future and bring it to our patrons.

Another way to justify adding a makerspace to your library is to take a look at how your patrons are using your collection and what they are asking for. If they are taking advantage of your computers frequently and asking for more computer training classes as well as other technological programming, it would be a fairly easy transition to take those patrons and introduce them to the world of the makerspace. Most of those patrons are going to want something to transition beyond computer basics. Why not give them something that will not only teach them about technology, but inspire them to think creatively and construct projects and patterns? Encourage them to develop ideas that have been in the back of their heads for months or years, but that they never fully knew how to bring it into fruition.

The idea of creating a makerspace as just another extension of collection development is beginning to emerge in the literature: "Libraries pride themselves on the breadth of their collections; perhaps the same principle should be applied to the environment as well. The library could look at its spaces as collections on their own: a library with as many designers as authors" (Goldenson and Hill 2013, 26). It is a new and possibly difficult concept to grasp, as collections are usually concretely defined as library holdings that have a circulation policy attached to them. But once we begin to see the library space as part of those greater collections, it becomes clear that we owe more to our patrons than just the traditional collection. Libraries need to offer more than just a storage facility for books. They need to cite reasons beyond the traditional advancement of learning and knowledge to get people not only to come to the library, but to stay as well.

Libraries need to start embracing makerspaces not because they are the latest and greatest thing on the market, and not because they do flashy things with futuristic technologies, but because "the better argument for acquiring a 3D printer is that libraries have adopted the role of providing universal access to technology over the last couple decades" (Library Technology Reports 23). Librarians who see *makerspace* as a buzzword are right—this *is* a buzzword at the moment. But the makerspace movement also shows signs of having lasting roots and will be desired by patrons in upcoming years. Just as personal computers were once new and rare in libraries, they are now commonplace; it's hard to imagine a library landscape without them. And for many services, the library is the only source for people in the community. Currently, 3-D printers as well as laser cutters and other makerspace technologies fall outside the realistic budget of the average hobbyist. By purchasing these items for our patrons, we can diffuse the costs and spread them out to a realistic price point for most users, who may only need to use the technologies for one or two projects. It is not our role to determine why our patrons need to use or should use certain technologies; we need only to provide these things to them so that they *can* use them. Just as Ranganathan said in his five laws, "Every book its reader," perhaps we should view technology in this way, with every technology its user (Ranganathan, 2006). If this is how technology is shifting, we need to start shifting ourselves and finding a way to offer these opportunities to our patrons as well. Resisting the inevitable only casts a bad light on libraries. By embracing the future on our own terms, we avoid having to wait for others to dictate to us what we should be doing with our own institutions.

Starting the Discussion

To start, make a clear rationale for why a makerpsace is needed and how it will benefit your community. Your library director will want as much information as possible about what to expect from implementing a makerspace, and with work and determination you should be able to develop a plan of action suitable for the library. A few essentials to begin discussing with colleagues are staffing and funding (explored more fully below), as well as the necessary materials and the projected number of patrons who will use the space.

Funding a Makerspace

Finances and budget are one of the first concerns libraries have when it comes to implementing a makerspace. It is a natural impulse. Even if your library is 100 percent behind the idea of a makerspace, things can quickly become derailed by the realities of a library budget. A few main sources of income for this type of project are familiar to many institutions: funds can be reallocated from existing library budget lines, grants can be applied for and received from outside sources, and donations can be requested from the community. Each of these has their individual merits and downsides. An analysis of individual methods follows.

Library Budgeting

Most libraries run on a fiscal year from July to June, so it can be important to know when to time a request, as funds are usually lower in the spring and early summer because the funding for the year has already been spent. On the same hand, there may be general funds that can be drawn for special projects, particularly one-time purchases and unique library-related programming and funding. Think creatively and try to think of any potential budget lines that can be drawn from. This might be a good time to get in good with your acquisitions friends or your director by quizzing them about what type of operating lines are out there and which routinely have extra funds in them at the end of the year. By getting an idea of where to expect funds, you can have a better idea of what to build your plan off of. Depending on your library, this might be public knowledge, and you can research what historical budgets have been and try to get a sense of what to expect from your budget.

Grants

Grants are a classic source of funding for many libraries and can provide a welcome relief to any library looking for extra funding for projects. They can come in all sorts of price ranges, from small funds in just the hundreds of dollars to massive funding sources that go into the thousands and sometimes much higher. The trouble many people have with grants though is that they can be difficult to find as well as to apply for and receive. It is a process that takes many months and a good deal of extra effort on the part of the librarians attempting to build their makerspace together. While it does take up time and a lot of effort to write up the specific grants, the financial help often makes it worthwhile. These grants can be federally funded or privately funded through your institution or another source.

Now is also a particularly good time to try and get a grant for a makerspace, as many funding agencies are receptive to new ideas and your library might have a better chance at securing special funding opportunities. One pitfall of relying exclusively on the use of grants for funding is that they are not always continuous; they are often one-time funds that can be used only for specific areas. This type of funding can also require the library to monitor carefully where each dollar goes so that they can justify whether the money was spent appropriately. Others are not as strict in enforcing how the money is spent, but these aspects are good to keep in mind during the grant-writing process, to help you decide whether to fund your makerspace completely on grants.

Grants.gov is a great place for librarians to get started learning the process of how to find a grant as well as to apply for one. It is important for those searching this website to be aware that as a government website, it provides only federally funded grants for you to search for. There is a world of grant opportunities out there, but if you stop at just one site, you will be limiting yourself from using some very valuable funding opportunities. Other sources such as ScanGrants.com allow for you to search a wide array of fields; while your library may not have an immediate connection to one particular grant or field, you may find sources that would not have immediately occurred to you that do have some overlap with the project you are trying to fund. When searching for funding resources, it is best to do broad searches, as money can turn up in unexpected places.

Because many makerspaces try to emphasize how they relate to STEM fields (science, technology, engineering, and math) and encourage children to go into these fields, consider looking into grants devoted specifically to STEM. There may be more than you had considered—and many worth dipping your toes into. If your only searches consist of simple *librar** for funding, you will not necessarily find much, if anything relevant. Searching for grants requires thinking of all options that could possibly connect or reflect back positively on your project. Many larger foundations like Carnegie, Andrew Mellon, Ford, and Sloan all provide numerous grants throughout the year which can be competitive but lucrative for those who get the eventual grant awarded to them. The trick to finding these grants—because they are not all in one common database to search—is in keeping in mind your searching strategies and using keywords such as *"non federal funding"* or *"library grants"*. Many libraries also publically announce who funded them in years past. It is worth seeing who has done similar projects funded by grants and see if there's another grant open this year. Many academic institutions also have a development officer who is paid to look for grants for you. Larger public libraries sometimes have a development officer available to them through their city government, but it is not as frequent. Try to explore all potential avenues when looking for a grant.

Writing a grant application can take several months; pay attention to the wording of the application, which often provides strict guidelines. Grant applications often require you to include a strict budgeting system as well as a fair amount of facts from past history and current use to prove to the grant approvers that you have a justifiable need for this grant. If the grant is not approved the first time around, be sure to keep all the information you saved and wrote, as it can often be reformatted for other grants and funds with a little effort.

Donations

Donations and gifts in kind can be an extremely helpful thing for a library. While most book donations are frequently hit or miss, a good director or dean will spend their time championing the library and its special needs to potential donors and figures in the community. Although many donors choose to give books or simply cut a check to the library, it can be worthwhile having an itemized list of specific needs in mind. The money is certainly helpful and appreciated, but keep in mind that larger donations often come with stipulations and requirements for how the

7

funds can be spent. Sometimes the donor wants it to be spent only on technology or only on books, while the library stares at other more desperate needs that could use the funding on better things than new books. With specific itemized requests, the library can ask for either the exact model of 3-D printer that they want or that the funds be donated specifically for their upcoming makerspace. Among so many options it can be hard to choose, and while you cannot make a donor do anything she does not want to do, you can make suggestions to them to help her in the donation process.

Looking for donors who want to help out with the makerspace can be difficult, but keeping up enthusiasm for the project both at work and in your personal life are important. Donors do not always appear in just the library environment. By having connections with the community at large, you can talk with joy and enthusiasm about your library and its needs while at baseball games, grocery shopping, church, or any other public space where you might come across a potential donor.

One emerging way to gather funding that has slowly started to trickle into the world of libraries is that of crowdsourcing. The Mesa Public Library used a modified version of this through their iMesa program, and other libraries have successfully used Kickstarter to fund their programming. Kickstarter is a website where anyone can help pledge money to fund creative and independent projects that might not otherwise be able to receive loans or other sources of funding. The Antelope Lending Library in Iowa City used Kickstarter as a way to raise over $20,000 for the library to lease a space for their local students. Although the space did not reach its ultimate goal, it did get enough funding to purchase and run a bookmobile and contribute greatly to the space (Schwartz et al., 2013). If your library cannot get enough funding from traditional funding sources such as those mentioned about, it might be worth looking into nontraditional methods such as crowdsourcing. Your library might have limits on ways that you can receive funds which could impede using Kickstarter and other crowdsourcing websites, but if these restrictions are not in place, it might be a very valuable tool for you to take advantage of. After all, it is certainly not unusual to receive a gift in kind or other donation that has severe limitations and restrictions on how that gift or money can be spent. Libraries are used to finding way to spend money appropriately while still following any restrictions.

Fees

The cost to use a makerspace varies, with most libraries opting not to implement a fee for patrons to use the space. Certainly it costs a lot of money for any library to implement a makerspace, but it is not unique or apart from any other space in the library. It costs a lot to build a DVD collection or a computer lab for a library, yet hardly any libraries charge for use of these materials. The primary purpose of a library is to provide free or low-cost services to their patrons, and charging for the use of these collections goes against those general principles. So many libraries are bringing the same ethos to the makerspaces by ensuring that they are low cost and are aimed at lower-income patrons who would not otherwise have the opportunity to play with such cool technologies.

Most surcharges have been made under the rationale that using a 3-D printer is analogous to using a paper printer or a fax machine. There is ink and paper—or in this case, filament—used, creating a solid object that can be taken away and does not have to be returned to the library. Rather than giving the item away gratis, libraries are charging for the cost of the filament used. This is usually done by the ounce, and is not terribly exorbitant unless the patron is making a massive project, which is usually rare. Most people using the 3-D printer so far have been curiosity users—people who make sample projects to see what they are capable of, but who are not in search of something unique and overwhelming.

Items such as 3-D printers are the first obvious cost that comes to mind, but there can be other options that libraries should consider charging a fee to use and attend. Particularly, any instruction class on how to use technology should be debated as to whether it needs to be assessed a fee. These library classes on technology have been implemented by many libraries for years, but they do take up the time and resources of the library with prep time and one-on-one training for large groups. A moderate fee could be easily charged for each student who chooses to attend the sessions. This would support staff continuing to teach the classes as well to help fund the technology that they work with in the labs, but again base this price on how many students you actually have and what your financial needs are. If the library does not offer a lot of technology classes and staff can generally fit these classes into their regular schedules, it might not be something worth charging a fee for; whereas if the library is teaching so many classes that it is slowly becoming a full-time job for the librarians teaching the classes, it might be worth adding a fee to the classes. This does not have to be anything overwhelmingly expensive. In fact, it probably should be on the lower side, just enough to cover expenses on the part of the library.

Allocating Funding

Determining where funds should go after you have acquired them can be tricky. Take a look at the core values that you want to bring to your makerspace. Will it need physical renovations? Technology upgrades? Staff salaries? Be aware of what will be a one-time purchase and what will require continual funding, and set your priorities based on these discoveries. Another thing to keep in mind is whether you really need something in your makerspace or whether you just want it because it seems like everyone else has it in their makerspace. Do not feel obligated to purchase something you will not use just because you feel like your makerspace will not be complete without one. If you do not truly need a 3-D printer and do not have any plans to use it in your programming, do not buy it! It really can be that simple. There is no set list of must haves for a makerspace. Ideally, all purchasing should reflect an end goal for a use that will be in place for a long time to come.

Many libraries have relied on smaller items that can be used by many for a long period of time, because of these reasons. Some continual orders you might need to keep in mind are that printers will require filament and software upgrades as time goes on. Additionally, many apps used for iPads and tablets will be current only for a few years, and your library might find that there is a need for a newer and better one in a few years' time. While often these apps are relatively cheap at just a few dollars apiece, if you have multiple iPads that will need to be updates, remember that these relatively cheap costs apply across all the library's devices, which can make even a relatively cheap application become expensive. While these costs will be relatively small, they will be costs that you can anticipate. Likewise, for computers and recording technology, your patrons will expect a certain standard of equipment, if not the newest. Be prepared to upgrade the software on these computers as well as to change out the hardware over the coming years. Hardware should not be expected to last much longer than three to five years; software can vary from program to program, but expect a shorter cycle, around one to two years.

No firm budgeting rules exist to create a makerspace, as each one will differ slightly, but if you consider your core sources for funding and keep itemized lists of where the money will go after you have received it, and then the library will be in strong starting shape. Create a list of your essential needs for a makerspace and itemize the costs and sources for receiving the items. Similarly, create a list of most desired programs and see if these two lists co-align. If you find that there are differences between the two, try to resolve them by figuring out what is most important for your space. Is it the technology that you are desperate for, or do you have projects that extend beyond your budget or capabilities? For some libraries, it might be easier to build the list of required software around the list of desired programs—that way a more efficient list of desired products can be built around what is planned rather than struggling to create programming around the machinery.

In the end, what you want are projects and technology that can fit within your budget and still meet your needs. Libraries with limited budgets may not want to think of this as an all-at-once project, but rather as something that they can bite off in small chunks. Start with just one project that requires the least amount of funding, or something which is already within your reach. Ideally this would be a one-time purchase and not something that would require continual purchasing. Build up that project and see how the public reacts to it. As time goes on, you can continue to add to this nascent makerspace with each new fiscal year or as gifts and donations arise. Just because you have a makerspace does not mean it has to be perfect and fully functional on day one. The goal and ideal of makerspace is to show continual progress and growth. If the library wants to slowly build onto theirs, it is certainly possible and to be recommended.

11

STAFFING

Staffing the makerspace is a key factor. Who will be expected to run the space and be in charge of its needs? Will these tasks take away from their regular duties at the library? Some libraries have only one person dedicated to their makerspace; others have a wide range of people associated with the space. This will vary wildly depending on how many patrons you expect to use the space, and also upon the types of projects you will be using for the space. Some projects require heavy supervision and guidance, while others will only need a minimal amount of supervision, with just one staff member pausing to check in from time to time so that they can show patrons how things operate (or perhaps just where certain items might be hiding). In some cases, creating a makerspace may require that you hire a new staff member. You can estimate your staffing needs based on how large your population is and the types of projects you want to have your patrons create in the space. You will also want to consider seasonal and peak-time variations; for example, it would not be smart to staff a children's space during school hours, or to neglect a space during summer break.

On the same note, consider how much training you want to invest into the management of the space. If only one person on your staff is able to run the space and know the ins and outs of all the machinery, the space will depend entirely on that staff member. Should that person become sick or quit, the makerspace will be effectively stalled until a new staff member can be trained or hired to replace him. It is good to have a backup for situations such as this, with at least two or three members moderately trained to know some information about the same equipment. Also consider that when there is a diversity of staff trained in different modules, general knowledge can get diluted, with one person becoming known as the "3-D printer person" and another as the "Arduino person." Sometimes this situation cannot be fully prevented, as everyone has natural skills and preferences that will come about as they learn; but if there will be a full staff for the space, try to ensure that everyone has a small working knowledge of the space so that single functions don't get relegated to just one staff member.

PROMOTION WITH SOCIAL MEDIA

Most libraries have limited options for how they can market themselves to users. Often, massive marketing campaigns are out of reach for the average library due to funds or simple scheduling. Most staff members just do not have the time to put extra effort into designing a well-thought-out advertising campaign. Often for those running a makerspace programs, marketing is just one project that they have to work on among many others. So in order to effectively spend staff time and energy, marketing has to come from quick and easy sources such as Facebook or Twitter. These are resources that will reach a great number of people with a small amount of effort. The reasons for this are logical and intuitive.

As social media becomes more pervasive in libraries and the world around us, it only follows that many makerspaces will begin to adopt their own social media platforms to use. Social media often forces libraries to interact with their patrons in uncontrolled ways that they might not have experienced before. The perceived privacy and anonymity of the Internet can often lead people to act differently online than they would in person. It is important for any library planning on using social media to have policies and plans in place for unexpected events such as these.

Throughout the book there are many examples of libraries that have social media accounts set up for their makerspaces and libraries. Most frequently used are, as mentioned, Facebook and Twitter. These commonly used platforms allow for libraries to quickly send out messages about anything from a change in hours to upcoming events.

Libraries that specifically use it for their makerspaces have found that they receive an uptick of "likes" and "retweets" from users, with a correlated uptick in attendance. While there are certainly many, many other social media platforms, these are just two of the most frequently used ones, in part because libraries are trying to contact their users where they hang out. Other major platforms that you might consider adopting are Google Plus (G+), Tumblr, Pinterest, and Instagram. Taking a brief survey of your user population to see what platforms they use most frequently can also be helpful in determining what platforms you end up using.

Ideally, your library has a social media policy or guidelines in place that you apply to your efforts in promoting the makerspace. Before you set out, your team should have a consensus understanding of your libraries' answers to the following questions.

What will we post?

- What is the purpose of your posts? Are they to alert patrons to your hours? To entertain them? To be a part of the conversation? These are all questions that need to be addressed before you begin posting.

How often will we post?

- Hourly, daily, or weekly, you need to find an appropriate schedule that will keep users interested without losing their attention.

Who is in charge of posting?

- Is this going to be managed by only one person in the library or will there be an entire team devoted towards crafting posts and managing responses?

Who will respond if something occurs during nonstandard business hours?

How will you deal with problematic patrons/posts?

One question is whether you should set up separate social media accounts for your makerspace or use existing library accounts. The choice depends on how often you feel that you can maintain an individual makerspace account versus allowing a larger library entity take over.

What should you post? Social media is a highly visual medium that thrives on the current and immediate moment. Some ideas for things you might consider posting include photos of events and the finished projects from your makerspaces. When showing off examples of the work created from previous events, you build excitement for future events. Patrons will not be able to come to your past events, but they will be on the lookout for future events so that they can attend those and do something similar to what you have previously posted. Much of the purpose of social media interactions is to drum up a community engaged with their library. The community will remember to use the site as way to find vital information, but they can come to recognize the library as a friendly and fun place that also offers a makerspace.

Some libraries adopt social media policies to dictate how they post to social media sites, including how often and what type of content they wish to publish. Policies such as these can be helpful for those libraries and librarians who are unfamiliar with the landscape of social media. It gives everyone a framework for how they are expected to interact on these sites. Sometimes, though, the gaps in these policies can create unforeseeable gaffs and errors. One potential way to avoid any pitfalls is to be hyperaware. This includes responding to all comments, even if it does involve negative feedback. Other things to consider are that social media is not something that follows the rules of the business world—people do not stop posting and reacting at 5 p.m. on Friday. People can and do comment at any time of the day, be it weekday or weekend. It is important that libraries have someone who is equipped and capable to handle any of these comments and reactions swiftly, even if the events might not happen during the typical workweek.

SUGGESTED USE: WHO SHOULD USE A MAKERSPACE?

A few main approaches to using a makerspace are commonly applied. Most libraries tend to dedicate theirs either to children, teens, or adults. Rarely do all three groups intermix in makerspaces. Part of this is based off of the different skill sets that each group has. Obviously an adult will work at a much faster pace than a child, but other concerns come up as well. Programming for a makerspace is tricky enough to plan for just one group; if a library attempts to program for three distinct age groups (or more!), they suddenly have a lot of work on their hands. Many libraries allow for parents or guardians to come and monitor or help with their children as they work alone, but such programming is not directed specifically at the adults in the group.

One group that you want to pay particular attention to when designing your makerspace is those with disabilities, so that you can provide them with full access to your collection and space. Helpfully, the Americans with Disabilities Act has provided guidelines for buildings and public spaces so that you can prepare for how to design the space accordingly. While this can be a very long list of items—which you should go over in depth before preparing—there are a few things which you might not immediately consider that can be vital to preparing your space for everyone.

First off, consider computer terminals that are at a height that those in wheelchairs can access or that are more open allowing for the wheels to have better mobility. While not all the computer terminals have to be at this level, provide enough to give at least the opportunity for disabled patrons to take advantage of them. Other issues to keep in mind are to be aware of the spacing between aisles and computer terminal banks. While easy to put into place, it can often get overlooked in the planning stages. The width between the aisles needs to be enough to let a disabled person maneuver through without obstruction. The minimum requirement is 36 inches, but the preferred distance is 42 inches. Try to keep these numbers in mind as you go about preparing to build and assemble your space.

ADA guidelines address physical accessibility, but another practical matter to address is figuring out when to offer programming for all. In any community with many different needs, no one ever has the same schedule. Students have slightly more predictable hours, with their free time primarily after school hours and on weekends, but even they can have conflicting afterschool activities that do not mesh well with the library's open hours. Adults work during every imaginable shift, and when they are not working, they are frequently carting their children home from school or other after school programs. Everyone leads busy lives and so it becomes difficult to assess when the best times for a makerspace program to run can be.

When trying to take into account all these varying schedules and needs, remember your library's base operating hours. In an ideal world, the library could stay open late for everyone and allowed everyone to work together on a come as needed basis, but this just is not possible for your sanity and continuity for others. Choose times that work for most people even if that means leaving off some people that you were truly hoping to reach. If the programming is a priority for them, they will find the time to come to the classes. The majority of public libraries schedule their programming for the makerspaces over the weekends, particularly on Saturday mornings. Afternoons are also commonly preferred times for makerspace times, though these are usually held on the weekdays for people who are unable to come on weekends, and so that children can stop by after school. Frequency of the programming will also be a big determinate of when you can schedule things. If your programs are only once a week, it's not hard to find the best times, but if you're holding programs every day, you will just have to assume that you will not get everyone there. It is an acceptable loss; not all programming can meet full capacity.

One way that libraries have found to get around some programming issues is to work together with local schools in order to have classes either come on field trips to the library or to have a librarian visit the classroom with a mobile makerspace. It can be a great method of outreach to your community that gets children interested and involved in their local library. Activities for these types of programs can either be ongoing, with the librarian visiting the classroom several times for a period of months, or just once. Either version works, but activities should be tailored to the time frame available to them. Working with teachers to figure out what their lesson goals are from the project can also help; it gives everyone a better sense of what to expect out of the children, as well as building a better lesson plan for the entire project.

Justifying whether your space should only be dedicated to one particular group is going to depend on how you plan for the space to be used. The pros and cons to making a space for only one specific group can vary, but ultimately you have to choose a model for your library space. While it can help teenagers or children to have a spaces special to only them, it can be limiting to other groups who might also want to participate. Another major issue to defend when specializing is why that one group deserves a majority of new technology and money when other groups suffer from lack of funding or support. Not everyone can get an equal slice of the pie in the library world, so if you want to go toward specialization, make a strong argument for your case. Demonstrate a justifiable need and show why your group needs the space over other groups. It can be all right to concede on small things, but hold firm to your original purpose: that of devoting a space solely to one group. Sun Tzu wrote, "Ultimate excellence lies not in winning every battle, but in defeating the enemy without ever fighting." While one should not look at negotiations to get a makerspace as a war, his methods can be applied to the business world well. Try not to engage your directors with a "We must have a makerspace or else!" type of argument; rather, try to see things from their perspective. You will be able to not only communicate your needs better, but perhaps understand what they will be able to concede on and what are absolutes for them.

Due to their structure and type of programming, makerspaces will definitely draw a certain type of patron into their doors without staff having to put too much thought into attracting them. The trick is in bringing in those who might not naturally be drawn to going to a makerspace. From the outside looking in, it can be difficult to understand what a makerspace is and this is a major hurdle for libraries to get over if they want to invite others to the space. STEM fields have become connected with makerspaces as a way to introduce younger children to the subjects and grab their interest before they get too old and think that they cannot do some of the things involved with STEM. In particular, girls have been a key target for these programs, believing that more women need to be brought into STEM fields to better represent a rounded view of the fields. A quick Google search on *girls and STEM* will yield millions of articles embracing the topic to the point where it becomes almost a buzzword. How does one build their library makerspace to bring in new patrons and fulfill all these high-minded goals without sounding like a buzzword machine spewing catchphrases and nonsensical words?

One key way is to do it with subtlety that involves focusing on the events happening during programs and not to stress what changes and transformative moments the events will bring about. Focus on things that create and modify, and find direct ways to appeal to girls without relying on blatant sexism. Makerspaces do not have to be dressed up in pink and glitter in order to bring girls into their folds; just show them how they can apply the things they create to other areas of their life. This will, of course, varying by the product being created, but it cuts girls short to sell them on the idea of makerspaces purely by pandering to their perceived tastes. Give them new ones, and you might find some repeat patrons.

Whether your library limits the use of its makerspace to just one group or its open to all, focus on making them accessible to as many patrons as possible while still maintaining your own guidelines and not bending over backward too much. Concentrate on core requirements and build out from there by trying to see who is most interested in the project and tailoring things to their needs. There are many unique ways to alert the public that you have a new makerspace open to them, but frequently, people want to rely on what works.

REFERENCES

Goldenson, Jeff, and Nate Hill. 2013. "Making Room for Innovation." *Library Journal* 138, no. 9: 26.

Ranganathan, S. R., P. S. Sivaswamy Aiyer, and W. C. Berwick Sayers. 2006. *The Five Laws of Library Science*. New Delhi [India]: Ess Ess Publications.

Schwartz, Meredith, Stephanie Klose, Caroline Lewis, Norman Oder, and Bob Warburton. 2013. "Crowdfunding the Library." *Library Journal* 138, no. 9 (May): 14.

17

Library Makerspace Profiles

ANCHORAGE PUBLIC LIBRARY

Anchorage, AK
www.muni.org/departments/library/pages/default.aspx
Remote Public Library

Located in the central part of the city, the Z. J. Loussac Public Library—the main branch of the Anchorage Public Library—has created their own makerspace for the citizens of the city to take advantage of. It is a brand-new project for the library that they are hoping to premier in 2014. What follows is how they have chosen to start setting up their space, along with their development process and ideas.

CREATION

The impetus to create this makerspace started with a greater renovation plan for the entire library, which begins in 2014. Each space in the library is getting an overhaul, with some areas being taken out completely and some new areas being added in their place. As plans for the final renovation came into focus, staff at the library realized that they needed to include a makerspace as part of the conversation, and eventually they realized they needed to include one as part of the renovation.

The unique part of this is that the idea did not originate with the library; rather, it was born out of the community. Members of the community brought it up to library staff, who then brought the idea to planning meetings. The Anchorage Public Library is lucky to have a dedicated and involved group of patrons. It was through discussions with these patrons—about what they liked and what they thought was missing—that the idea to create a makerspace came to Paul Baker, the library's Innovation Lab coordinator. Baker researched ways that libraries were incorporating new technology, and he felt that a makerspace would be a natural fit for both what his patrons were asking for and what they were capable of providing.

This is truly a homegrown space. Since the idea came from the community, the members can consider it their own place, not something being imposed upon them by the library.

PHYSICAL SPACE

The location of the makerspace at Anchorage Public Library is located on the top floor of their four-floor library. It has a beautiful view of the Chugaik Mountain Range, which the staff feels will inspire innovators as they work on their individual projects.

The positioning of the space was not chosen at random. The room on the top floor is removed from most of the quiet spaces in the library. The library wants their users to have the ability to make as much noise as they wanted, without the fear of being shushed by either the staff or one of the other patrons. The space is 100 feet long by 35 feet wide in its own room, with a few offices in the back. By placing the space up here, staff have yet to receive any complaints about noise. They avoided this potential problem by considering all the possible locations and problem areas, such as areas that needed to stay quiet and areas where patrons would be more likely to tolerate noise. Initially staff spent time on the third floor below with their ears strained for any noise spillover, but none was heard. This makes them cautiously optimistic that they will not have any noise issues in the future.

Regarding how many users can take advantage of the space at any given time, the library anticipates that the space can accommodate up to sixty people at a time, with an ideal of thirty people per session working on hands-on projects, as well as staff members to assist.

The space needed some renovation; they did not build it completely new. This space was the library's former media center, so while it has been a subtle upgrade in some ways, they are planning on making it a more useable makerspace for their patrons, beyond simple computer access. They replaced the carpeted floor with something more industrial and capable of taking a beating (as well as capable of simply enduring more foot traffic than the previous carpet could have handled). In addition to the new flooring, they are also adding new counters for workspaces, along with new tables that can be used as collaborative workspaces. Rather than reusing furniture, they are choosing new furniture specifically for this location so that both the flow and function of the room will work well together. This would help to make everything look intended and not as though the room has been thrown together in haste.

TOOLS

Choosing what types of machinery they would add to their space was done through conversation and rationalization with their budget from select members of the staff. In the end, some of the key pieces of equipment that they chose were 3-D printers, Linux (which they use as the main OS at their lab), Apple and PC computers, some Arduino kits, and—for a touch of fun—Lego and Erector sets.

Arduino Kits

One note on the popularity of Arduino kits: many libraries have chosen these kits to include in their library makerspace programs. For those not acquainted with the kits, they act as open-source hardware on small microcontroller boards. Typically users can program anything on the boards and "teach" their projects to do a wide variety of things. It gives people a hands-on opportunity to see the inner workings of a computer, as well as directly manipulate how they work. And the individual kits are extremely cheap for personal use: most cost under $100, with many costing much less. Given the skills that such kits can offer and their relatively low cost, they are a natural choice for many a budget-conscious library. In addition, their low cost allows for the library to invest in multiple kits for large classes to use simultaneously, rather than having one unit that may or may not be checked out at any given time.

Operating System

Linux is a popular operating system for those who want to build their own operating system and choose how things will run on their own individual machines—so it can seem like a bold system choice for the Anchorage Public Library. Their rationale for choosing Linux is that they were able to design their own build with a team of local volunteers. Linux is, after all, a free option among many other proprietary operation systems. Even more amazing, their entire operating system can be run off of a flash drive, so the library hopes that when makers are using a specific program or are used to using Linux, the makers can go home and boot it up on their own computers using a flash drive.

One of their intended programs is to have computer donation drive, to give makers the opportunity to refurbish their own computer with a Linux operating system. The Anchorage Library has focused on bringing tools to the library that will give their patrons a hands-on learning model, where they can learn by doing things directly rather than to be lectured or read to without actually getting to try it out for themselves. Many maker programs rely on this DIY approach to teach their patrons, because they feel the spirit of the makerspace invites patrons to learn skills either by themselves or with the aid of guides—so that patrons can take these skills outside of the library and into the community at large.

PROGRAMMING

Currently the Anchorage Public Library is still in the process of coming up with programming ideas, but they already have a few ideas in store. They have hired a maker-in-residence who will be able to work at least part time at the library and help individuals as they come up with ideas. The maker-in-residence will be expected to come up with a number of programming ideas, and ideally will have a core project that patrons can always return to (and that will boost word-of-mouth regarding makerspace programming). This maker-in-residence is not in charge of the entire program, but will act as a leader of the space, helping give direction to what types of ideas can be successfully executed.

Current Classes

Already the Anchorage Public Library has several successful programs that could easily be adapted to their makerspace environment. In the spring of 2012, they had a very successful program for their Science in the Library program, "Plants and What They Need," with science-oriented games, crafts, and activities focused on teaching young children what plants need in order to grow. These are ideas that will likely be incorporated into future makerspace programming. Another program, offered to older patrons, is computer classes for common issues that these patrons may run across, such as how to make a listing on Craigslist, set up an e-mail account, or use Microsoft Word or Excel. As these classes are typically held in their computer and media rooms, they make a natural leap into the makerspace environment.

The goal, however, is not to simply renovate the media room and give it a new name. Rather, the library is making this a space that is open to everyone regardless of age or any other limiting factor. This is truly a space for everyone, and ideally they will take these more established classes and grow them into newer offerings that can be adapted to the makerspace environment.

MARKETING

Cheap and effective library marketing is one of the factors that many libraries rely on to get patrons through the door and into their programs. Often libraries do not have the budgets for expansive marketing programs, so they have to look around them to see what types of programs are available to them. This is the case with the Anchorage Public Library, which relies on cheap and effective social media to help them spread the word about their events and activities. They have found that many of their users are also using the social networking sites—and users actively encourage the library to tell them about hours and events that may be coming up in the future.

The library has Facebook, Flickr, and Twitter (@anchlibrary) accounts. They have several thousand followers on their Facebook and Twitter accounts, and these followers actively participate by liking and retweeting posts. The library's marketing plan for when the makerspace fully opens is to invite participants through use of these social media tools, slowly drumming up news and support. Likewise, they plan to use other traditional mediums for marketing, such as flyers by key library access points, newsletters, and the always-handy word of mouth. All these methods of interaction with the public offer the library relatively cheap options for spreading word about events—methods that have proven effective in the past.

So while a big part of the library's marketing planning is based around social media, this does not mean they have excluded traditional methods of marketing. Although these are less trendy marketing methods, they should not be overlooked, simply because they are effective and have proven success rate. Keeping these things in mind, the Anchorage Public Library has chosen these methods to get their message across when the time is right. Ideally, this will be a few weeks before the official opening of the makerspace; that way they will be able to drum up some hype for the big reveal. The library wants people to be eager to attend the grand opening, so they will need to generate excitement for the space before it actually opens. The library does not have a real sense yet of how many patrons to expect to be using their space, but they want to be ready for as many as possible. As of this writing, they have already begun initial preparations for marketing the space. Of course they are hopeful that they can drum up a good amount of buzz.

STAFFING

Although the library has several great plans for getting up to speed and renovating all around, this does not mean that they have the funds to hire a lot of new staff members to help out at the makerspace. They have chosen to rely on volunteers to help staff the new makerspace. In their ideal world there would be about three volunteers in the space during peak use times, but this will likely vary based on availability of volunteers and their schedules. As for the skill sets of the people volunteering, the makerspace needs people who are capable of adapting quickly to new technologies. While they are not required to know everything about each new technology as they come out, they will hopefully know a thing or two or can learn and pick up things with quick skill. For example, they want people that already know how to operate computers and can troubleshoot when things start to get sticky.

One of the key people in helping to set up the makerspace at Anchorage has been Paul Baker. Educated at Lindenwood University, he works as the Innovation Lab Coordinator at the library. The Innovation Lab is designed to help local community businesses develop and grow (Alaska Public Media), and from working there Paul has applied the skills he has learned there to what he wants to bring to the makerspace. One of his chief goals with the space is to ensure that it does not become snagged in the belief that the space belongs to only one group of patrons such as children or teenagers. He stresses that the space will be open to anyone who wants to participate. He wants this to be an open space for everyone in the library. Although many of their users are older and looking for jobs, they believe that even these users can take advantage of the things they will offer in their makerspace. It takes a bit of a hopeful attitude as well as natural promotional skills and talent for him to take advantage of this opportunity.

When a library's choice to create a makerspace is driven by staff, it involves being aware of the surrounding library environment. While many of the ideas and projects might not be practical for you or your library in the initial stages of creation, they do help to lay the foundation or future projects. Some of them will be very helpful, and when the timing is right—whether you learn about a project at a conference, through a trade magazine, or just networking with colleagues—you will know how to bring the idea to your library.

The Maker-in-Residence

A few other libraries have begun to implement maker-in-residence programs at their libraries, and Anchorage Public Library is one of them. Because many of these makers-in-residence are working for a substantial amount of time for their libraries, they are often hired as library staff or given one-time consulting fees. For the libraries that cannot afford to finance another line in their budgets, of course, this automatically defeats the idea. There can also be issues with determining how long a maker-in-residence should stay at the library. While some libraries are content with hiring a maker-in-residence indefinitely, others choose to rotate their makers to get a variety of projects as time goes by. Although this can be nice for the patrons and offer different perspectives and viewpoints, this also puts a new onus on the staff of the library to find new makers to replace the old makers. Usually a library requires a several-month commitment from their maker-in-residence, so while they might be able to find people who want to serve, those people simply don't have the time to participate fully. Similarly, even if a library can find someone who wants to be a maker-in-residence, he might not want to teach the type of things the library can offer or wants to offer.

When libraries can find makers-in-residence who want to help them out, they are very grateful; but for the reasons listed above, not all libraries choose to take this path. In addition to this, sometimes the library has a staff member already hired who can offer the same level of expertise. This is partly because many times, staff members who bring up the concept of a makerspace are some form of maker themselves; whether that involves simple projects or highly skilled things, they tend to be people who have always embraced methods of creativity in the library. Having an in-house maker does not make or break your space, but it is an option for those libraries with the funding to consider.

DEMOGRAPHICS

The type of users at the Anchorage Public Library does not cover as wide of a spread as the typical public library. The average user for them is in their mid-30s to 50s and is a job seeker. With these things in mind, the library wants the makerspace to be a place for everyone to use for a wide range of purposes, not just job seeking. Yet they want it to reflect tasks that can help their job seekers. The Innovation Lab is one area where job seekers can learn about the ways of business and what to expect in a job interview or how to build a résumé, but the overall aim for the makerspace is to get the attention of all areas of the population. They want all ages. So they plan to include everyone, from young children all the way up to their eldest patron. The space is defined as a place for the young at heart, and they have chosen materials that they hope will bring out that aspect in all their patrons.

Forms

Before the Anchorage Public Library even opened the doors to their makerspace, they took a look at what other libraries across the nation were doing with their own. They wanted to look at simple things such as projects and machinery as well as some of the more hidden details—how the spaces were running on the backend. (As we all know, small details about policy and mission statements are things vital to any library space but often get overlooked until they are needed.)

During this process, the Anchorage Public Library began to notice that many libraries were implementing permission forms for their patrons to submit before taking advantage of their makerspaces. The library considered all the technology that it wanted to implement in their space, as well as all the possible risks that they could incur by letting their patrons use these materials. Eventually they decided that they wanted to implement a permission form for their patrons to use before they enter into the makerspace. Although the library does not anticipate that anyone could get hurt from their makerspace—after all, they view it as a safe space—they do want to make sure that it remains that way. One of the rules that they ask their patrons to follow is that all young children under 8 be accompanied by an adult. This is for a few reasons. It keeps unsupervised children from getting lost and potentially hurt, and it also gives these young children someone to turn to and give them an added hand during hands-on activities that can be slightly difficult for those still mastering fine motor skills.

■ ■ ■

The Anchorage Public Library is still very much a library in the state of flux. They have had a bunch of changes in the past year—and they anticipate even more to come—but they are doing so while embracing the future. Reasoning that they cannot remain in the past, the Anchorage Public Library has tried their best to see what types of innovation are taking place around them, and have taken that knowledge and applied it where they see best. Sometimes this has meant doing things on a smaller budget than they would have dreamed about, and sometimes they have gotten unexpected windfalls (such as through volunteers who helped them with creating Linux-based computers and other services). This has been a true community based operation for everyone involved in the creation of this space, since day one.

If you want to bring a makerspace into your library environment, be prepared to work collaboratively and take advantage of the opportunities presented to you, even if they come in unlikely forms and shapes. Libraries do not have to be completely redesigned from head to toe in order to add makerspaces. They just have to find a little room to play around in.

27

REFERENCE

Alaska Public Media. 2013. "Big Plans for Anchorage Public Library Headquarters." March 14. www.alaskapublic.org/2013/03/14/big-plans-for-anchorag-public-library -headquarters/.

BROOKLYN PUBLIC LIBRARY

Brooklyn, NY
www.bklynpubliclibrary.org
Public Library

The Brooklyn Public Library system is unique in that it has a huge population to serve: over 2.5 million residents and several branches, all offering something tailored to their individual needs. Few libraries have to serve populations as large as this. Based in a large city where they have a broad and varied user population, the library has tried to think of unique ways to meet the needs of everyone. One of their most recent innovations is the Shelby White and Leon Levy Information Commons, which functions as their de facto makerspace at their central location.

CREATION

The idea for a makerspace at the Brooklyn Public Library was not merely a jumping-on-the-bandwagon sort of thing; it was part of a strategic plan hatched by the library and spread out over many years, going through many phases. The plan was first put into motion three years ago and will likely carry on for many more years to come.

One of the core pillars to this strategic plan recognizes the need for digital literacy among the library's patrons. Digital literacy is increasingly become a much-needed skill for those who want to be competent in the workforce. Building upon other forms of literacy, the aim is to get users comfortable with digital technology—not so that they are experts in all mediums, but rather so that they feel comfortable using new media as they approach it.

The pillar of digital literacy is, of course, only one of the library's goals for the rest of their community, but they are using the makerspace as a way to meet one of those pillars, just as they are using other parts of the library to meet other needs. These pillars or goals are to provide: education, access, culture, inclusion, space, and stewardship for their community at large. The Brooklyn Public Library has over sixty locations throughout the borough, which gives them a wide range of targets to meet these goals with. As at any major public library, there is no typical patron; they vary wildly from branch to branch.

FUNDING

Through a generous $3.25 million grant from the Leon Levy Foundation and a grant from the federal Recovery Act, the library was able to contract Mori to create their spacious 5,500-square-foot commons. The Leon Levy Foundation has the ability to cover some operational costs, but once the grant ends, the library will need to absorb the costs of operating the Levy Information Commons, for which they have begun to prepare.

Fees

The library does not currently charge patrons to use the space. At the moment, all classes are free to the public, and they anticipate that this will remain in place for as long as it is financially possible to offer classes for free. For the most part, the library was able to afford the costs of the space through their grant funding, and very little of those costs had to be passed on to the patrons. This is in part done through careful budgeting and planning, but also because the librarians at the library did not want their patrons to have to pay to use the space, as they felt this would unnecessarily place burden on their patrons and even in some cases hinder those people who might truly need the space from using it. This goes back to one of their pillars mentioned above, of access. A core belief is that everyone should be able to use the library space, and so they need to be able to provide access to materials that they might not otherwise get the chance to use.

PHYSICAL SPACE

Finding the space for a makerspace can be tough. Much of the equipment involved takes up a lot of space; even if it is not being actively used most of the time, it still requires storage. Similarly, there can be sound issues with the spaces, as often things such as the 3-D printers and group work on projects can create noise disturbances that most patrons are unaccustomed to in a library setting. Many libraries take spaces that they already have available and try to find ways to repurpose them so that they can turn them into makerspaces, but the Brooklyn Public Library had the luxury of hiring the world-famous architect Toshiko Mori in early 2012 to help design their new information commons. Having worked on projects across the world, Mori has a style marked by a sleek modernism that incorporates nontraditional materials, such as polyester and fleece, into the traditional.

After construction was completed, it was time to fill the commons with the new makerspace and other sections that they wanted to bring to the library to the opposite sides of the library. The space is immediately visible as you walk into the main doors of the library; the glass walls even allow you to see through the space. There are three general sections within the space: a workspace with public seating and desktop computer workstations: the lab, which is used for classes and other programming, and finally the meeting rooms, which includes six general-use spaces and one recording studio. Each section within can host a large number of people at any given time. The workspace can hold seventy people, the lab holds up to thirty-six, and the meeting rooms are designed for a maximum of forty-four people. If all spaces were in use at once, that would be an impressive 150 people all working on projects at once.

The space is designed to have a bright, open, and airy feel. It has a clean modern look, as if you are in the library of the future. Although open, the meeting rooms in the space and barriers in the room create natural divisions that give each area its own unique setting.

The space includes twenty-five specialized computers for users to do a variety of projects. This consists of ten iMac designing stations, thirteen Hewlett-Packard research stations, and two Hewlett-Packard design stations, each with varying limits on how long users can use each machine. The library also purchased some unique machinery specifically for their recording studio: microphones, cameras, and even a green screen so that patrons can create all sorts of audiovisual works. These were basics that they felt were necessary for a recording studio. It was an interesting transition, as the library had never before offered access to materials such as these. There was a learning curve regarding the appropriate uses and time lengths each patron could use the space and machinery for. It was important for the staff to establish these guidelines and boundaries early on to establish precedent and teach users how they were expected to use the space.

Creating Room

Though the library was lucky enough to have a world-famous architect come in to help them design the space, even they were not immune to trying to find a unique space for their new information commons. The space was constructed where they had previously stored their Popular Library collection, comprising such materials as DVDs, CDs, audiobooks, and periodicals. In order to make room for the space they had to move the popular library collection to a smaller space upstairs, as well as moving machinery such as microfilm readers and general use computers to other locations throughout the building. The library decided that it needed to make this a top priority, and so they spent much time looking at usage statistics and also weeding through their popular library collection before they moved it to another level. This took considerable preparation and thought, but in the end it seems to have panned out well for everyone. Initially there was some confusion as users came to the library expecting to find these materials where they had always been, but after an initial introduction phase everyone learned about the new spacing of the library and came to accept the new changes.

TOOLS

Choosing the right machinery for a makerspace can be incredibly stressful. After all, these pieces of equipment are expensive, and not only the cost hinders libraries, but for most libraries it is likely that you will have to live with these pieces of equipment for a long, long time. Ideally a library should plan on a renovation lasting a decade, and as mentioned in "About Makerspaces: Concerns and Considerations," equipment lasts two to three years apiece. In practice, of course, this can be hard to actually do. To entirely replace all your computers at once can be a huge financial burden, and likely renovations will only come on an as-needed basis and not as recommended. How can a library know when they are likely to have the funds or grants to replace these old pieces of machinery again? Often grants and funds can come through suddenly for one-time purchases that must be spent quickly before they disappear; this creates the added stress of needing to find the right piece of equipment quickly—and for cheap. Some libraries try to build funds into their budgets for recurring costs so that they will always have the funds to purchase new computers and technology. Even a large library such as the Brooklyn Public Library is not immune to the challenge of finding good equipment to fill a makerspace. They knew they needed Mac computers in their information commons. Although the price of Macs can be more per computer than PCs, they felt that the ease of use and audiovisual production programs on the machines made it worth the purchase cost. (Some of these programs included iMovie, After Effects, Photoshop, InDesign, and Illustrator.) They also relied heavily on the advice of their IT staff when they were purchasing audio equipment for their recording studio, particularly because these staff members have specific audiovisual responsibilities with the space and would be the ones most likely to help when it came time to fix the machinery.

For software, the library staff had a somewhat easier time of choosing the appropriate programs to install on their new machinery. They wanted to have a good mix of proprietary and open-source software for their patrons, in part because they want patrons to be well versed on every type of software, and also to give the public a chance to take advantage of programs that they could not otherwise afford or justify the purchase of.

PROGRAMMING

The Brooklyn Public Library offers a wide range of classes on any given day to their patrons. The topics can vary wildly, from the basics of computing to the more complex issues of teaching patrons about digital media education and ways to take advantage of the recording space. These are all regularly well attended by the general populace, with classes usually reflecting many different ages and types of users. Although some of the classes are specifically directed at age groups and markets that may not have as much computer experience as others, the main goal of this programming is to get everyone interested in computing and creating as much as possible so that one day they can take greater advantage of the other things that the space has to offer.

The library has outsourced some programming to the BRIC Arts | Media | Bklyn, which is a local organization that runs the borough's public access station, among many other cultural and media activities. They were chosen to present some of the harder classes because the librarians wanted to offer the best to their patrons, and there was the general consensus that they felt that they were not adequately trained or prepared to offer these classes themselves. This may change as time goes on and staff begins to feel more comfortable teaching the classes on their own, but for right now, they have a happy relationship with the BRIC Arts organization, and no immediate plans to cancel their relationship with them.

One of the most well-attended programs is the weekly Teen Tech Time, which gets teenagers acquainted with gaming and other technology. Some classes are for budding game designers—the basics of how to build custom video games as well as other options.

Classes

At the moment there is no one unique project presented to users when they go to the Brooklyn makerspace. The library offers a wide range of classes so that when people walk away from the classes they bring with them the skills to create something entirely unique to themselves, and they can later on take other classes that add on to the skills that they first learned at the library. Not all the classes are designed to be built on top of one another—they cover a wide range of topics—but the idea is that they should all flow together from a basic level of understanding to encourage people to make and create. Each session begins with the basics and grows up from there, allowing participants to learn programs from the ground up. Topics have included everything from how to use a green screen to how to import video from camera to computer.

Some classes do have prerequisites so that teachers do not have to spend time on extreme basics. Generally these prerequisites require students to be familiar with the basics of using a computer, such as using the mouse and knowing how to open files in the start menu. These classes run at all times of the week, though they do try to offer more classes in the evening and later hours so that they can accommodate working professionals.

An added benefit to these classes is that anyone can sign up for them through the library website—an easy registration option for those who wish to join in. Patrons can still sign up for these classes in person, but the majority of attendees are signing up now through the website. This is encouraging news for those staff who were unsure of how to market the classes, as it gives them a better grasp of reaching users online.

MARKETING

Due to the size and nature of this makerspace project, there was a fairly intense amount of marketing so that people would be made aware of it and know that it was open to the public. There were web announcements for the grand opening, as well as print flyers and social media discourse. The library was lucky in that they have a whole marketing department, which allowed them to take some of the tasks from the regular staff. The library decided to approach the marketing from many different angles so that they could get unique community populations in to use the space. The makerspace idea was pitched to some local publications and weeklies so that local residents could be made aware of its opening; from there, local blogs picked up on the news, and it began to spread that way through word of mouth—or word of blog, as it were.

Social Media

There is a dedicated Twitter account for just the information commons (@bpl _infocommons), and as of this writing they have over two hundred followers. Although this is a relatively small number, they are expecting it to grow as they expand their outreach. They frequently post photos of their space in use, showing students and other patrons learning new things and taking advantage of the space. The photos show a clean white space with modern furniture, as well as projects with students working individually on laptops that have been provided to them through the information commons. The library's use of Twitter offers a sense of fun, with the librarians tweeting about new furniture and discussing the process of setting up the new space (and thus building hype).

The next step for the Brooklyn Public Library is to find specific individuals who can spread the space's message even better. Some of these individuals include filmmakers, independent journalists, artists, designers, and other creative types. In part, this is so these very creators know the space is available and can take advantage of it—they can then take the information and spread it to others in their field, thus encouraging use and getting the word out to people who the library would have previously had no means of contacting. (One benefit to the space's location is that it just so happens to be located in a very prominent and central part of the library, so most visitors to the library learn about it at some point.)

STAFFING

The information commons at Brooklyn is staffed through a variety of ways. Most important, thanks to grants they were able to fund stipends for five part-time intern positions. Through these workers, the space is staffed during most of the hours that it is open. The library also keeps a reference desk staffed during operational hours, and this is used as an additional service point for when the makerspace is busy.

A variety of staff members—not just librarians—conduct classes in the space. There is no one single person in charge of the space; it is just a space that all areas of the library try to take advantage of. This may change as ideas solidify regarding how to use the space, but for the moment, everyone seems to be peacefully coexisting—which is a great sign.

Community Involvement

As previously mentioned, the space also includes BRIC Arts | Media | Bklyn, but the library is always on the lookout for more partners, and they have an open invitation out to anyone who wishes to be a workshop facilitator or instructor. They do have some parameters in what they will accept as instructors. They ask that all applicants send a history of what they have previously worked on, as well as a full lesson plan written up for what they want to teach in their classes. This is all part of keeping an open attitude for how to take advantage of the space. Many people working in the library want the Shelby White and Leon Levy Information Commons to succeed, so they actively look for people who also feel the same way and want to add to the space in a positive manner. No one person controls the space, but everyone hopes to contribute to it and help it grow.

35

DEMOGRAPHICS

The Brooklyn Public Library has an incredibly diverse population that they need to give attention to. Collection development is focused on unique areas, but staff have to address the needs of a wide group of people who do not necessarily share the same outlook with one another. The Information Commons is currently no different. The library has chosen not to restrict makerspace access based on age level or any other limitation; the space is open to anyone who is open to learning. The space is labeled for the general adult population, with a few programs that have been marketed specifically to the young adult population segment.

The space has a very steady usage. The library reports that they have people in the space all throughout the day and evening when they are open. Generally between one and three classes are taught there every day, and when these classes are in session, the usage rises to a higher rate. Statistics on the recording room are still coming in—it is the newest portion of the space, having opened in January 2013—but on most days it has at least one reservation, sometimes many more, so the staff are encouraged and believe that as the space becomes more widely known, there will be more people taking advantage of it and sending out information on it.

Forms

At the moment the library has opted not to create any type of release form for users taking advantage of the space. They feel that this is not needed due to the fact that the type of machinery patrons use is not likely to cause major physical harm. Only a few libraries have chosen to require forms (usually makerspaces that have small children working with the 3-D printers, which could understandably cause some harm if the children are left unsupervised).

■ ■ ■

The spirit of the Brooklyn Public Library makerspace is to expose patrons to new technologies and explore their creative side so that they will have the opportunity either to create at a low cost something that they would have had to pay much more money for, or to learn skills that they never knew they had. The library wants to prepare their patrons for future jobs where they might be working with particular technologies, or just to offer their patrons a place where they have particular equipment to learn on.

Whether or not makerspaces prove to be a fad within the library community, they do resonate with one of the main purposes of libraries: not only to preserve culture, but to offer culture to those who cannot get it any other way. As society continues to shift toward technology, we need to acknowledge that technology is a part of our cultural heritage, which should be preserved by the library.

Through this space, the Brooklyn Public Library has chosen to address the needs of its patrons by first making a strategic plan and assessing what is needed most by all their patrons, and then trying to figure out what is tenable from this. What makes this makerspace so successful is not in the types of materials that they chose, but that they were able to come together as a community and build something that could be used and appreciated by everyone. There was much thought put into it, highlighting that what all libraries need to do before undertaking the task of creating a makerspace is to consider deeply what things their library truly needs in order to succeed. Now that the space has been implemented, the Brooklyn Public Library can sit back and watch the fruits of their labor blossom, and hopefully it will continue to be successful for many years to come.

CARNEGIE PUBLIC LIBRARY

Pittsburgh, PA
www.clpgh.org
Public Library

When The Labs at Carnegie Public Library were launched in 2012, nobody was quite sure what to expect. The Labs encompasses four locations throughout the many branches of the Carnegie Public Library. Based within just the city of Pittsburg alone they have a population of over three hundred thousand people to cater to, and the surrounding suburbs are factored in, the needs only become more amplified. The Carnegie Public Library approached this by starting with a strategy of bringing their makerspaces to as many locations as possible, and it has only grown from there.

CREATION AND FUNDING

Money for the project was entirely grant funded, and the library's plans for future funding are also based on projections for being grant funded. They used some ingenuity in using resources they already had on hand so as to do some of it on the cheap, but they still were responsible for bringing in a great deal of expensive equipment. In relation to this, the idea for the mini labs was born through a discussion with the MacArthur Foundation—specifically, the YOUMedia Network and all the specific projects that were taking place in libraries across the nation. As the library discussed the specific creations and projects with the foundation, a makerspace began to seem like a natural fit for the library, and so they began to set to work on creating one of their own.

In relation to this, the mini labs are free for the teens to use, and they intend to keep them free for as long as possible. They only anticipate costs being based around upkeep of the electronics and other makerspace materials. These are not the type of costs that they wish to pass on to their users, and so the mini labs remain free.

PHYSICAL SPACE

The Carnegie Public Library has chosen to place their makerspaces at four separate locations. At the main library, the first makerspace is located in the Teen Department, two others are at the East Liberty branch and the Allegheny branch have labs that can be rolled into meeting rooms, and then at their South Side location they have a loft space upstairs that they take advantage of. Due to the wide range of size and type of material, each mini lab or makerspace has its own unique feel and uses. Programming can vary from each different location. Each of these spaces is aimed at teenagers and their development in the STEM fields, and is part of a larger whole. Over the coming year, the library has plans to develop and redesign all their teen spaces to better include teenagers, as well as to incorporate these new mini labs.

Noise Issues

In many makerspaces, noise can become a major problem. Sometimes the problem is based on the acoustics of the library which can easily carry sound, or sometimes it is based on the machinery used in the space, or even just because of the excitement of users who are talking too much while building things in their makerspaces. At the various branches of the Carnegie Public Library, they have yet to encounter any major noise problems with their labs. There are a few reasons for this. At three of their locations, the labs are held in private spaces where teens can work together, away from the rest of the library patrons, and the walls serve to block out sound. Staff have yet to receive any complaints from patrons about teens or machinery creating too much noise at these new spaces.

However, at the main library location, they have had a few noise issues, but they are not the typical sort caused by the machines themselves. The noise problems that they are having with the main library branch are caused by the fact that it is on the first floor of the library, which is not a dedicated quiet area. Anyone is welcome to talk on this floor, and so the noise problems are largely from other patrons rather than from those who happen to be using the makerspace at the time.

As this ambient noise tended to break the concentrations of teen patrons—and as the teens had a few projects that required total silence—staff brainstormed for a bit before they came up with the idea to purchase a recording studio for the space. Because soundproofing is vital for recorded projects, this gives them the much-needed silence for their teen projects, alongside with the added opportunity for patrons to record almost anything that comes to mind.

The recording booth is one of the few things that they had to buy in order to add to the existing spaces. As with budding makerspaces, the library's general space implementation was a homegrown affair, making use of many materials that they already had available, such as spare chairs and tables for furniture. The spaces were often in unused rooms or places that had been shifted to accommodate the needs of the new labs. In the case of the main library, most of what they had to add was just shelving, storage, and equipment, along with basics such as bulletin boards, as well as whiteboards that would be used while giving instructions or teaching a lesson.

These are not spaces that require a lot of money. You can very easily take the existing spaces you have, add a bit of equipment and watch the creativity spring out from your students.

Repurposing Space

At the main library, the space that they repurposed was the "study area" of the Teen Department, but it had never really been used for this purpose. It is the area farthest from the reference desk—and in large part because of this, the loudest area. So it was a welcome alternative to take a space that was not really fulfilling its purpose and turn it into a space where teens could truly do something productive, and would want to hang out.

At the other locations, the library has taken advantage of existing meeting rooms. These rooms can still be booked by regular members of the community—staff just reserve the rooms for special projects and then roll the materials needed in on a special cart. Their only concern with these three branch locations is making sure that the equipment is stored in a safe and secure location when it is not in use. As these are smaller items that can be more easily picked up and carried off, they are naturally things that library staff want to pay closer attention to. Their plan is to keep them in storage cabinets under lock and key so that staff knows who has access to the cabinets and keys at any given time. So far they have not had any problems with this system.

STATISTICS

Since the arrival of the mini labs, the staff of the Carnegie Public Library have been watching usage statistics, naturally hoping to see what kind of interest there was in the spaces. Staff have mixed thoughts on how to interpret them; it is important for the library to differentiate between those who are actively using the space and those who just happen to be there. Just because users are in a space, doesn't mean that they happen to be taking advantage of it in the ways the library wants them to be.

On most school days, the main branch of the library will see a huge crowd of kids after school lets out. Usually this is between forty to fifty kids at once for around an hour or so. Not all these kids take advantage of the makerspace, though of that group, they usually have about five to ten regulars who will really engage with the space, making use of the various elements set out for them. Having a steady influx of users from the local schools gives the library a great user base to rely on, with an average minimum of fifty users of the makerspace per week—often more.

These stats are only for the main branch downtown. Individual branch libraries have noticed other types of usage. Their numbers are not as high because they do not have the large dedicated space that the main branch does and they cannot hold events as frequently as the main branch does, but they do have encouraging statistics to report. Their workshops regularly draw three to eight people per group. Initially they were discouraged by these low numbers, but they report that group sizes are becoming larger as word spreads, and they now have more staff mentors on hand to manage the workshops and assist teens with their projects. When they first started running the workshops they did not have any idea of how many people to staff the spaces with, or how much of their attention would be needed for each user. These needs will be addressed later on in the chapter, but they do see the demands on their spaces going up as they place more attention and focus on it.

TOOLS

The spaces have had to rely on smaller-ticket items rather than on the larger ones that many people come to associate with makerspaces, but rather than seeing this as a fault, the staff at the Carnegie Public Library have chosen to address this with creativity and drive that makes their mini labs a force to be reckoned with. Some of the items they have chosen make sense; for example, they stocked their main library branch with iMacs and iPads to give their students computer access. But then they got creative and thought beyond just standard desktops. They began to purchase up many unique apps for the iPads, and they also bought a PlayStation 3 and an Xbox 360, plus the game Minecraft, reasoning that the gaming stations would help to bring students in as well as to teach them to think creatively—particularly with Minecraft, which allows users to create their own cities and worlds.

Other purchases included conductive thread/LED craft kits, a Nikon DS3100 DSLR, Canon Vixia camcorders, Adobe CS6, and Adobe After Effects. All these things were chosen through a thorough process of the library considering their hopes for the space and considering the needs of their users. The staff talked to others in their "community of practice," read user reviews, took suggestions from their own patrons, and finally consulted their budget to determine what items were the most needed. Nothing they purchased was done so on a lark. Everything was considered with the intention that all the apps and technology should be able to not only help their teens, but also encourage them to come to the library and give them a fun space to learn and play in.

PROGRAMMING

The makerspaces are open six days a week at the main branch, and currently only one day a week at each branch location. They also have a plan to include extra "Open Lab Days" at branches as they are able to in the future. The library has set up a weekly schedule for their Main library branch that stays mostly the same throughout the year. Creating a reliable schedule has been helpful in allowing people to know and predict when they can come in to use the space. It tends to look something like this:

- Mondays—Music/Audio Day
- Tuesdays—Design Day
- Wednesdays—Maker's Studio
- Thursdays—Photo/Video Day
- Friday—Free Day
- Saturday—Wildcard

The main library holds a workshop based around the theme on the day of the week. So on a typical Monday, a workshop would be designed around creating a music- or audio-based project, as opposed to a Tuesday, where the workshop would probably be based around designing plans be they architectural or creating plans to create a robot.

The programs have become very popular among the students, but the things that have become most popular are the lab kits. These are smaller items that teens can check out to create a wide variety of things.

41

One of the most important factors that the staff at the library tries to stress is that using technology can be fun, and is for everyone. They do not want to limit things to just boys or just teens in certain grades. One of their most popular workshops is Hip-Hop on L.O.C.K. (*L.O.C.K.* stands for leadership development, organizational skills, cooperative economics, and knowledge of the music business.) Using the space's budding recording studio, this workshop includes a live session with a local DJ, a writing session to help the teens learn how to put their ideas down on paper in the best formats, and hands-on training using top-of-the-line recording instruments. The workshop runs several times at each location and runs in the afternoons for about three hours.

Training and preparation for the events can take a considerable amount of time. Staff need to find time to coordinate events with any potential guests, such as the DJ, as well as to make sure that their lesson plans are in place and understood by all staff working with the teens during these workshops. This particular workshop is held at all the branch locations. While not all the locations have specialized recording studios, they all have unique apps on their iPads and other media lab stations that can help the teens to work together and create.

The accessibility of these programs is also helpful, because more and more often teens either have an iPad of their own or have access to one. By being exposed to the programs at the library, they can learn how to bring these ideas back home and continue to work at home. (The apps that are loaded onto their machines are generally free or low cost, so they are not something which the teens would not have the ability to access on their own.)

The Hip-Hop on L.O.C.K is only one small sample of the typical programming held at the library each week. Referring back to their previous schedule, this workshop would typically be held on a Monday but could also appear on a Saturday, their wild card day. This scheduling and programming are both part of a great way of encouraging teenagers to take advantage of their library.

Not every activity in the library has to be a direct studying or learning activity. The space also offers gaming days, where teens are encouraged to come by and play on various gaming consoles against staff members. The main goal is to present the library as a fun place to hang out, with the long-term goal of presenting the library as a space where teens know they can go to for a wide range of needs.

MARKETING

In the case of the Carnegie Public Library, staff have used signs to direct people in the library to the specific location of the labs. This helps when people know that the space exists but do not know exactly where it might be. Staff have also used the major social media platforms to alert their followers that they have a new space or just simply to alert them about specific events that will be taking place in these mini labs, acting as a motivating calendar, encouraging followers to come participate with them.

The library has also made a point to send mailers out to the local schools letting students know that the programs exist, in the hopes that teachers and administrators at the schools would encourage their students to do their school projects at the library and take advantage of the materials available to them there. They also rely on direct outreach and word of mouth in the community. The staff has been deeply pleased about how well word of the spaces has spread—people are always trickling in saying they have heard good things about the place, and want to take advantage of it.

One of their first major projects was the QuickFlix project, where teens created their own short videos using the video technology at the labs. They did a great deal of promotion to market this event, and they had eighteen final entries submitted to the contest. The library posted these videos on their YouTube channel, on their own website, and even as links of individual entries on their Twitter account. By doing so, they had a great spread of potential users watching the videos. Their hope is that when they run the contest in the future, even more people will be aware of the program and teens will return again and again, in the hopes of doing better and potentially winning. (The winning entries can be seen on their website: www .clpgh.org/teens/events/programs/quickflix/.)

The library tries not to worry too much about how many people view a particular video or tweet. Instead, they hope to get the message out—slowly but surely—that the makerspace exists, allowing for steady, manageable growth. While they are not yet at maximum capacity in terms of how many teens can use the space at any given time, they do want to keep manageability in mind. Many of the staff seems to like working with smaller groups because it grants them the opportunity to work closely with their students and grow personal relationships with the teens.

STAFFING

Each makerspace has a unique staff that aims to make the makerspace learning experience fun and interesting. These staff members are informed about their technologies and able to troubleshoot minor problems that might arise before having to refer to the IT department. The main library branch has four part-time mentors, along with the digital learning librarian, who primarily work in the space. Each of these mentors take turns leading workshops, and each has their own area of focus that they specialize in; however, all are equipped to deal with any part of working in the makerspace. Staffing at the other branch locations relies on teen volunteers who can assist in the programming whenever possible. For the most part there is fewer staff to help out at the branches—often only one or two people running a workshop there.

When any teenager approaches the mini labs and asks to participate a few things will take place. On their first visit, the teen will be asked to register with either their library card or an ID, and then one of the makerspace staff guides the teen around the lab, giving them a brief tour and simultaneously introducing them to the policies and procedures of the space so that the teen knows what is expected of her. These are procedures that only take place during the first visit to the lab. After the first visit, teens are expected to remember and follow the rules. They are always welcome to come up and ask for more guided help and instruction with certain projects; for the most part, they are free to use the space as they wish after the first introduction. The teens can use their library cards to reserve time at the computers, and generally this helps reinforce the process of using the space.

DEMOGRAPHICS

As with many public libraries, it is hard to define the "typical" user of the Carnegie Public Library, but they define themselves as a large urban public library, and so the user type comes from a broad range of economic and educational backgrounds. Sometimes when a library attempts to bring in a makerspace to the library, patrons can have a difficult time understanding the concept; they struggle to understand why it is being put in place, and more often struggle just to understand the basic concept of what a makerspace can be. At the mini labs at Carnegie Public Library, there was almost the opposite problem: teens in particular seemed to get the concept almost instinctively and were eager to take advantage of the opportunities there.

As the program grows and develops, staff have noticed that some of the teenager's ideas of preconceived conceptions of what a makerspace is have shifted and realigned somewhat. This is in part due to the efforts of the staff at the library advocating for the space, as well as for the students who have watched the programming at the makerspace and slowly figured out what type of events they should be expecting there. Since the programs and mini labs are so reliant on teenage users, the peak times for the space tend to follow a natural school rhythm and pattern, after school and on Saturdays at the main library. Staff anticipates that during the summer break, these peak use times will shift somewhat, but as of this writing, they have not figured out when those precise times might be.

Forms

The Carnegie Public Library has a blanket photo/permission form to use images and likenesses that they ask all their teen patrons to sign. In addition to this form, they also have a few special permission forms for when they have more intensive special programs. This is part of their larger library policy, which they have carried over to the mini labs. On their website and in internal presentations, the library has used photos of teens creating projects so they wanted to make sure that they wouldn't be held liable for this usage. The likeness form is not a strict "sign or do not use the space" form. Rather, the library wants to take into account that some people may have reasons to wish to stay private and keep their image and works off of the Internet, so they ask that teens let one of the mentors know in advance if this is a concern. The library keeps the rules to using the space fairly simple and posts them both online and on location at the branches. The rules are based on a general sense of respect for everyone in the space and are basic to follow.

CLEVELAND PUBLIC LIBRARY
Cleveland, OH
www.cpl.org
Public Library

The Cleveland Public Library has thirty-one branches spread throughout the city, as well as a bookmobile that regularly goes through all neighborhoods. They have a large service population, but their primary makerspace is located at their main downtown location. They came up with the idea of a makerspaceby asking "Who are our patrons? What skill level do they possess? What could our staff do? And why do we need a makerspace?" Since they first asked these questions, they have watched it flourish in a number of unique ways, with plans to expand upon their makerspace in the future.

FUNDING

The funding for the entire TechCentral department as a whole was budgeted from the library's general fund. They were lucky in that they did not have to go very far to get funding for the space. However, there were several smaller in-kind donations that were made to the library in time and skill by vendors involved in the development of the My Cloud system, in which they brought in consultants to work on the system, at their own expensive. It was a very gracious and kind donation, but for the most part the whole space has been funded entirely from the library without the aid of grants and federal funding. The library is open to applying for grants, but for the immediate future they plan on trying to keep most of the funding coming strictly from the library. Most of their major purchases have already been made, and from here on out they anticipate their primary purchases for the space to be maintaining basics like plastic and paper for their printers, and then general maintenance of equipment when their computers and other machinery need to be replaced or become too old to be repaired.

The library does not charge fees for makerspace use. However, they do charge their users for the printer plastic, as it can be very expensive to stock. The cost is five cents per gram of plastic, which is the same cost that the library pays for the material, so they do not make any profit off of these 3-D objects. Most objects that users end up creating are between $1 and $5 to create or between twenty to one hundred grams of plastic. Although your usage may vary, this is helpful to the library when trying to plan how much plastic and filament to buy. Knowing how many grams of plastic your users are going through in an average week, helps predict how much you will need to stock in advance.

PHYSICAL SPACE

The Cleveland Public Library has not set up a space dedicated solely to their makerspace, but rather they have a common meeting space in their TechCentral department termed the Flexible Learning space where many of their maker activities take place, along with many of the other traditional programs one would associate with such a space. The Flexible Learning Space encompasses approximately 7,000 square feet in an L-shaped pattern. Placed near the front entrance to this space is their 3-D printer which is conveniently placed there so that those patrons who happen to be walking by can be drawn in by the spectacle and come in to create something of their own and learn more about what a makerspace can be.

The Flexible Learning Space can accommodate up to twenty people comfortably while working on Maker programs, and many of their services can be used anywhere in the space allowing for many more people to use the space at any given time. The Flexible Learning Space had been an unused portion of the library, and they repurposed it with the makerspace in mind, but eventually they would like to create a dedicated space in the library for maker activities. Part of this is based on the success of the maker activities, and also just for scheduling concerns and questions this would be easier for them to process.

One of the most frequent problems the library encounters is differentiating between TechCentral and the Flexible Learning Space. They are both housed in the same environment and serve similar functions, but have key differences. Their funding even comes from the same source, so often the spaces can be confused, so signage has been placed to differentiate between the places as well as to stress the focus that while everyone is welcome to use both spaces, they should be aware of key the differences before attempting any major project—not to hinder the process of their projects, but merely so that they will have access to the right tools with as little confusion as possible.

Noise Issues

Due to the multi-functionality of the space, there can be some mild noise issues with the space. In part this is due to the fact that they have nearly one hundred public internet computers in the Flexible Learning Space, making the noise level in that area substantially higher than it would be in any other area of the library. The Flexible Learning Space is directly across from this area, and there is some noise spillover and carry over. At the moment they have no immediate plans to fix this problem as it has not yet become a major issue. The library takes a positive approach viewing it not as a problem in need of fixing, but rather as something which draws people in, as they want to know what is going on to cause such noise. This is a classic example of making the most out of a situation that others might have looked upon negatively. It is this cheerful spirit which helps create such a flourishing library environment.

48

TOOLS

Before they stocked their makerspace, the Cleveland Public Library knew that they wanted to purchase a few big ticket items like a 3-D printer feeling it was essential for many of the activities they were planning on using. They reviewed many of the printers on the market, but ultimately went with two options. They chose a MakerGear M2 as well as a MakerBot Replicator 2 as their primary 3-D printers, but alongside these printers, they also ended up choosing to purchase 35 MakerKits. These MakerKits were chosen because although big items like the 3-D printers certainly take up the glamour of many makerspaces, they also wanted to focus on simple making that was more approachable for the general user that may not have a giant project in need of a 3-D printer, but they did want to create something. These makerkits are comprised of the following items: 10 Korg Monotrons, 10 SnapCircuit Kits, 8 K'Nex Kits, and 7 Little Bits Kits.

Toys

Amid this array of new technology, you might have noticed a familiar name or tool. Some of you may have grown up with K'Nex Kits. The classic childhood construction kits were chosen because they would help patrons learn how to model and build realistic structures while still maintaining a fun atmosphere and because they are a tool that would be familiar and inviting to their patrons. Similarly, although they are not as old as K'Nex, SnapCircuits offer patrons the chance to create their own electrical boards and learn about the basics of creating circuit boards. Although these educational toys are designed for children, that should not scare off adults, because these things are designed to learn concept, and many users enjoy the opportunity to get to "play" while they learn. Each of these kits can be checked out and used anywhere within the library space.

When it came time to purchase laptops for their users, they have also purchased the unique My Cloud Thin Clients. These are laptop like devices that patrons are allowed to check out which accesses a Windows 7 Virtual Machine. The primary purpose for supplying these machines was so that when patrons need specialty programs for their projects, they would have a place where they could safely install these programs without harming their other machinery. The library was worried that if they offered other computers, there would be the risk of patrons inadvertently downloading viruses or other malware and harming the computers, thus leading them to purchase more or spend more time repairing them. This was something they wanted to avoid, so the My Cloud Thin Clients seemed like a natural choice for them to flock to. Many of their computers ended up using programs like Gimp, iLife, Audacity, Openshot, and the Microsoft Office Suite. These software packages were chosen specifically because they represented a wide range of products that could be created, but where also easy for patrons to use and still offered a great deal of tools for the cost. What made them eventually settle on the MakerBots was among other factors, going to a local company in Cleveland and visiting their makerbot and questioning the staff about how it worked and if there were any functionality problems.

This is a good technique for anyone to keep in mind before making a big purchase. If at all possible, find ways to check out the machinery in use and hear testaments from those who actually use the product. A product demonstration from a vendor can be nice, but ultimately lacks the ability to let you truly play with the features and see any potential real world problems that your library would be likely to come across, and a vendor might be hesitant to tell you about. Would they buy it again? Do they like it? What are problems that they have with it?

Once they had purchased the first 3-D printer, they ended up purchasing a second one from a different vendor under the idea that they could then give their staff experience in using different platforms.

The library does not want to limit itself to one type of technology, and would prefer that their staff knew a little bit of everything so that they can help their patrons with just a little bit of everything. For the Cleveland Public Library, it was vital that they make choices that didn't represent their own personal bias, but rather reflected what they felt their patrons needed and would appreciate the most. Hence, they chose multiple versions of 3-D printers so that there were multiple options for the patrons to choose from and get to know.

TechCentral has several unique components that also allow people to work together in groups. Tables have been provided in the room for group collaboration, but they have also put in some media components like a smart board for community members to display projects and work on without the aid directly. Smart boards are great features that remove the need for a mouse. A user can simply touch and point on the board, performing all the basic actions that the mouse would have otherwise provided. In addition to using the smartboard like a giant tablet, users can also use special pens to virtually draw on the screen, allowing for key bits of information to be highlighted and shown to a group at large. They make for great group collaboration, and seemed like a good resource for the library to add to its resources.

The library also provides a resource termed the Tech Toy Box, with iPads, Nooks, and Kindles available for checkout so users can explore these devices before they make a financial investment of their own, learning which models they prefer. Additionally, those who could not normally afford to purchase one of their own can use the devices; particularly because income should not limit people from taking advantage of technology, it is vital for the library to provide these tools to users in need.

One of the key components of the makerspace is that they have made themselves very aware of the need for more power outlets. Prior to the creating the space it was a common complaint for patrons to need places to plug in their laptops and other machinery requiring electricity, so they made sure that this new space would have power outlets all over and in well thought out spaces. It seems like a simple component, and certainly one that often gets overlooked, but it has proven vital to them when working with high tech resources that often require being plugged in to operate. Power outlets are an easy thing to overlook, but once a structure is in place they can be hard to add, so it can be good to think of these things ahead of time. Libraries should keep simple things like these in mind. While your library renovation may already have enough power strips, remember that there will be basic things that you take for granted that need to be accounted for. Leave no small thing unaccounted for, and keep room in your budget for unexpected changes and surprises once everything is in place, and you'll find that you have a great functional makerspace.

PROGRAMMING

A precedent was set that all maker events in the library would be held on the same days to establish a routine so people would know when to expect the maker activities to take place. Makerlabs are always planned for Saturday mornings so that they can bring in families. Between Saturday mornings and Monday mornings, they tend to have their peak usage of the space, simply because this the time when most users can take advantage of the space. They have users throughout the week, but they can predict that the space will always be busy over the weekends, whereas it is less predictable throughout the weekdays.

Classes

The library holds a number of maker activities and events, which one primary event being focused on each month, and each are variations on things that makers can create with their 3-D printers or other tools available to them through the space. Some of the program titles include: Custom Cookie Cutters (using the 3-D printer), Making Panoramic images with Photos or Video, Designing Your Own Font, Video Slideshow Creation, Digital Kaleidoscope Art, 3-D Printing with Thingiverse, and Photo Editing with Pixlr among many of the projects that they have done. The community has greatly embraced these things, because it allows them to work within their skill set towards something familiar and yet new at the same time. When they held their very first makerspace class, it was the Custom Cookie Cutters class, and they had nearly 30 people participate in the project, with all age ranges: children, teens, adults, and even seniors.

Statistics

As can be expected use of the space varies by day, but typically as a main portion of the library, the TechCentral space sees anywhere between five hundred to seven hundred people per day. Use varies by the normal factors such as weather, school holidays, and local events that bring people downtown. Now this space also encompasses the computer lab, but they also have other unique markers to let them know whether or not the actual makerspace portion of the lab is being used. For example, they have been monitoring how often requests for the 3-D printers are put in. They have seen these requests rising, with staff members printing off between five to seven objects per week for patrons, with some of these requests including multiple parts for multiphasic creations. The requests for the 3-D printers mirror the numbers of general users of TechCentral, which helps them determine what percentage of people are being drawn into the makerspace. They expect use of the makerspace to only continue to go up, as they have begun to receive more and more press.

MARKETING

The marketing for the Cleveland Public Library's makerspace can be divided into two types: primary and secondary. When the space was initially created they did a heavy rollout of marketing through traditional means like library signs, print media, and other ads. However, their secondary marketing has come to them rather favorably by their associations with many local organizations within the local community, which brings attention to the work that they are doing with the makerspace, and by association draws more people into their space. By having other media mention them without their direct encouragement that helps spread word of mouth, as well as providing them the backup of the company advertising them. If a patron trusts the first company, they are going to trust the opinions of that company, so that this trust gets extended to the library in return. However nice the secondary marketing is proving to be for the library, it was not a planned out portion of their marketing strategy. It was simply a nice kick back that ended up benefiting them. That said, other libraries can watch how the library benefited from these partnerships and try to simulate or recreate the same experience in their own communities.

STAFFING

The library uses their existing staff of 12 FTE to help staff the makerspace, although usually there are only 4 staff members in the actual makerspace to help out at any given time. Together they roam through the space looking for people who are struggling or have questions, or one of them may be guiding a class during a particular maker activity. It only varies by the day. Naturally, as the staff has gotten used to the machinery, each person has come to specialize and work better than others have on certain areas. Some staff members have become the default or go to person when it comes to working with the 3-D printers or on

My Cloud and the like, though there are other staff who remain generalized. It is a very democratic approach to using the space. There is no one person who controls only one area or demands that they have exclusive rights to the printer, but rather every staff member draws upon their own experience and tries to help others with what they can. The entire TechCentral area is thought of as another service point, and so staffing is figured out by availability and assessing what other areas of the library will be busy and in need of what services. It is a very sensible process.

The ideas for the makerspace came late in the game as they were in the middle of building their TechCentral space. The original idea had been to create a learning lab atmosphere were users could come in, use computers, and get specialized help from staff members who had a strong background in computers. Midway through the development of these ideas, they began to learn about makerspaces and quickly realized that the concept of this was quite adaptable to what they had planned for TechCentral. So they began to amend their earlier plans, and made sure that they could also fit into it a makerspace for creation and imagination. Before they had created TechCentral the space was a fairly flat multipurpose computer area that offered access to older computers and microfilm readers, but it lacked any real depth or incentive for others to come there. When they created the newer space, they wanted their patrons to have not only a reason to enter, but for it to be a place that was truly a place where people wanted to be and where they had access to the ability to learn together.

DEMOGRAPHICS

The makerspace is located in the heart of downtown Cleveland, which brings in a unique mix of people to the library. There are a few shelters close to the library, and for many of their patrons the library is their only source of internet access. On top of this they do have some teenagers who use the space in the afternoons, but as there are no schools nearby to their downtown location, they are not the primary users of the space. Some libraries will specifically target one area of their service population when creating a makerspace, but in the case of the Cleveland Public Library they took notice of who was using their library the most and would have the most need for a makerspace. As such, it turned out that the adults from the shelter as well as others were the most frequent users and so they have spent a good deal of thought in tailoring their works to the needs of their patrons.

One of the nicest and kindest things that the staff at the Cleveland Public Library have begun to notice in the makerspace is that people genuinely want to help each other. They have begun to observe patrons assisting other patrons to help get things working in the labs. Usually it is from patrons who have used the space before and are already aware of the ropes, but it is encouraging to watch people begin to work together without the aid of staff members. These are members from all walks of life, and part of what helps to establish a community. By taking people who have a common project to work towards, you give them an opening to get to know one another and learn about the things that make each other similar and unique. The makerspace has become an incredible bonding experience for family members working together as well as friends and strangers. Although it is not one of their stated goals for the makerspace, creating a sense of community embodies the spirit of a makerspace, because it allows people to learn from one another

New Populations

All of this is great programming, but one side effect of all the marketing and outreach that they have done through secondary marketing has started to draw increasing numbers from different populations than would normally come to their downtown branch. These new populations include teachers, college students, business people and inventors who come in specifically to use the 3-D printer and other makerspace services. Often they are doing these things for class projects or individual projects that they otherwise would not be able to complete without the aid of the library's 3-D printer. Having people from all sectors of the community come in at this point is certainly encouraging, but initially, it was tricky to convey the purpose of the makerspace to the community. Community members did not understand the idea of making. This was the primary purpose of purchasing the MakerKits so that they could help teach people about the idea of making. Slowly the community has begun to respond, and now they see regular use of all their maker materials.

Forms

Release forms vary by library and policy, but in the case of the Cleveland Public Library, they have chosen not to use release forms for those who use the space. The reasoning behind this is based on the fact that patrons do not have direct access to the 3-D printers; staff are the ones who handle the machinery and do the actual printing for their users. They feel that if the patrons are not directly using the machinery that they are most worried about, then there is not a need to create a release form for users.

With that in mind, they are planning on increasing the machinery that will be used in their makerspace to include equipment with the potential to get hot and have sharp surfaces. Once those pieces of equipment have been put in place, they plan on also including a release form for both the protection of the library and its users. So at the current time they do not use release forms, but once they begin to use equipment that requires them, they plan on implementing them.

■ ■ ■

In large part due to their successful marketing and use of smaller MakerKits to convince people of their needs, the Cleveland Public Library makerspace has really taken off. The staff are looking into new ways to expand upon their space. They want it to be an active learning space for all ages, and so they continue to look at new products and activities, searching for anything feasible to bring to their patrons that they could not otherwise gain access to.

GEORGIA INSTITUTE OF TECHNOLOGY

Atlanta, Georgia
www.library.gatech.edu
Academic Library

Located in midtown Atlanta, Georgia Tech University is famed for its strong emphasis on science and technology. With over twenty-thousand-plus full-time employees, the institution is a publicly funded research university. The makerspace in the Georgia Tech Library opened in spring 2013, and although new data is still streaming in by the day, since the first day it has seen continual use and improvement of the space, with new and unique projects taking place all the time.

CREATION

A wide-open space, the Information Commons at Georgia Tech is open twenty-four hours a day (with the exception of holidays). Before it became a makerspace, the commons had several things going for it, such as a media lab and a large plotter (a printer for vector graphics). These things were nice accents to the space, but a more dedicated source for creativity was needed. The idea for a makerspace was conceived when library was approached by the professors of the class GT 2303, titled "Your Idea, Your Invention," who were looking for a common space where the class could meet. The library immediately fell in love with the idea and quickly jumped at the opportunity, brainstorming ways to create a space that would be useful for students while remaining cheap, as the budget for this space was very slim from the outset.

For a library that already had an information commons, the evolution of that area into a makerspace can be a natural transition. These two types of spaces can be frequently confused and thought to be more similar than they are. Both spaces are needed and useful, but the confusion between the two can lead to questioning whether makerspaces are particularly suited for the unique environment of a library. Understanding the cultural differences between an information commons and a makerspace is key to understanding why such changes are important to the library system, and why makerspaces are needed in libraries.

Information commons spaces tend to allow for group and independent study with technology, yes, but one of the core differences between the two is that an information commons is not defined by any particular lesson or desire to create.

A makerspace's main objective is to teach and train users on how to create new skills and expand their knowledge of technical matter. So while the Georgia Tech library was happy to have an information commons, they felt it was necessary to expand its role into a makerspace.

FUNDING

The Georgia Tech Library relied upon special financial support from the Provost's Office, using what was in essence a furniture fund to fill their makerspace with new items. Although the library tried to keep their costs as low as possible, certain expenses such as furniture that could not be repurposed and printing costs came up naturally, and they had to seek funding for these from a few different resources, particularly the Provost's Office.

Fees

One of the benefits of the space is that very few materials are needed; it is seen as more of a coworking space than a materials space, so users are not charged a fee. If later down the line the library chose to implement materials that would be high cost, it might consider implementing a fee for use, but this would not be a profit turning enterprise, just something to cover the cost for the materials. Students who take GT 2303 still have to pay tuition to take the course, but they do not have to pay any additional lab fees. This can be a major incentive for the students considering the course, because student fees for classes can rack up very fast. The library, of course, had to pay for their own operating costs, but they choose not to pass this on to the students at this time.

PHYSICAL SPACE

Encompassing an area in their already spacious Clough Information Commons, the actual makerspace in the library is only about 700 square feet. Though relatively small by some standards, this space accommodates the needs of the library; at the moment they do not see a need to expand it. It easily seats twenty-two students at a time, with the potential of seating up to thirty students comfortably.

A variety of materials were needed to create the space. As with other libraries who chose a general theme of using surplus materials, surplus architecture desks were brought in, as well as shop stools and Z-Racks, which were custom built to accommodate the space. (Z-Racks are modified garment racks that, with the addition of basic showerboards, can become the common moveable dry-erase boards that we have all come to know and love.) The racks were put together by staff, and they have found that students—particularly those in classes—are taking advantage of them most.

The space was repurposed from the already existent group-study area. They first took out all the group-study tables and chairs, replacing them with readymade surplus material.

One of the purposes of the space is to be used as an idea incubator, which requires ample power outlets, cords, and wireless Internet. Use is not restricted to one sole group of patrons; anyone is welcome in the space so long as it is not in use by a class, and they actively encourage people to take advantage of the opportunities there. The walls are moveable, which gives staff the option to reconfigure the space to fit the needs and dynamics of various projects. Most of the time they do not need to rearrange the walls, but for special projects and events, it is nice to have the option available to them.

The space is in keeping with a modern library. The Undergraduate Learning Commons was just renovated in fall 2011, and although not defined as a library, it is attached to the main library and receives many of the same visitors. Lots of open airy spaces with desks and chairs clustered together create unique learning environments that allow students to work solo or in groups. The building was designed to be environmentally sustainable, and the design process shows throughout the building.

Noise Issues

During the creation of the makerspace, its placement seemed like a good idea, with designers reasoning that because the space would not be lecture based—and thus not a noise disturbance to the rest of the information commons—noise would not be an issue. Since day one of the makerspace's opening, however, the area has been plagued with noise problems. In part because the area connects to a computer lab without any barriers, noise is free to travel unencumbered. Part of the problem is caused by talk between enthusiastic students and teachers as they work together on projects, but often the noise can stem from the machinery they use as well. It is not an intentional disruption, but it is one that they had not considered when they were first putting the makerspace into place.

PROGRAMMING

Many makerspaces have a wide selection of activities and programs that rotate throughout the year to allow users to experience a broad spectrum of things. This Georgia Tech makerspace is unique in that a semester-long three-credit course—"Your Idea, Your Invention" (GT 2303)—is taught there each semester. As mentioned above, the concept for the makerspace came about as a way to support the class, but the library did not want it to be an exclusive classroom space for just those students and teachers; they wanted this to be a space for everyone to take advantage of. When class is not in session, other students are free to use the space as needed, but when class meets (often twice a week, for an hour and twenty minutes), the lab is closed as a dedicated space for those students. However, with the exception of GT 2303, there are no formal directions for how students can use the space. Future plans allow for more general activities and potentially club meetings.

GT 2303 actively meets there for only two hours each week, and in a 24 hour lab, that is a minor amount of the hours that library is operational. With this in mind, the library has helped create a makerspace that embraces its students and faculty, allowing for abundant classroom creativity—and not hindering other patrons who wish to use the space.

GT 2303

In the syllabus, GT 2303 is defined broadly as "beyond simple technology" and incorporates examples such as the U.S. Constitution, games, and symphonies. The sixteen-week course is divided into three parts, each based around a project of increasing difficulty. Teaching the course is a collaborative effort; eight individual professors from a wide array of departments across the university have come together to build the course. Departments represented include Mechanical Engineering, Digital Media, Computing, Industrial Design, Biomedical Engineering, the School of Public Policy, Electrical Engineering, and the Libraries. With such a wide range of fields represented, the hope is that students will be able to draw from all resources and make their own decisions in the creative process, which they might not be encouraged to do in just one field.

The first part of the course is built around teaching students to brainstorm ideas. In the second part of the course, students form into teams and test out making actual products and projects based on the ideas formed during the first part. Students learn how to create prototypes, design them, and validate whether they work. The last portion of the course—which is graded the most intensely—involves students carrying an idea to full term; at the end of the course, they have a high-fidelity version of their project to present to the class as a whole.

The course is innovative and relies on the makerspace greatly so that students can create full-scale renditions of their projects, as well as have a place that encourages them to develop their ideas and projects without interruption. The makerspace functions as both a classroom meeting space and as a learning lab, where students are free to test out ideas and see if and how they come to fruition.

As of this writing, no one project has emerged as the most commonly created one. Encouragingly, each student has had a unique vision for using the space, and there has been very little overlap. The professors and librarians note that students have come up with such a variety of ideas that very few of them run along similar lines. By the end of the spring 2013 semester, there will be a better idea of what types of projects students were most drawn to. The hope is that students create several prototypes throughout the semester that will help them learn about the design process from start to end product.

Competition

Unlike with many libraries, there is some small competition among makerspaces at Georgia Tech. The library is aware that they are not the only space on the Georgia Tech campus that is doing something like this. There is already a Makers Club on campus in the Engineering Department that has several active members. In order to create their own makerspace, the library needed to keep it separate and offer something unique to pull students into the library. While the Makers Club offers a wide variety of expensive tools that the library could not justify purchasing, the library can provide a collaborative learning space and get involved with other campus professors and officials to bring their blended courses to the library. So far there has not been too much fallout from the creation of the newer makerspace. While the Makers Club tends to remain on their own turf, the library makerspace is open to everyone, even those who are not a part of the class. In fact, this is a benefit to the library makerspace. The people who use and attend the library makerspace do not need to meet any requirements to use the space; they need only bring their ideas and creativity to take advantage of it.

Women and STEM

Everyone wants to bring girls and women into the discussion about STEM, and nowhere more so than at Georgia Tech, where only 30 percent of their students are female. Nationally, most schools have a more even split, with women often outnumbering men at 58 percent enrollment. (National Center for Education Statistics 2013). Women at Georgia Tech are more likely than their national counterparts to be in a STEM field. The library hopes to encourage this further with the makerspace by making STEM projects feel more approachable.

One argument is that women enrolled in a technical school have already been introduced to STEM and are already passionate about it, so why reach out to them? Most people agree that the time to reach women is before they have gotten to college. Yet such students may only be passionate about one STEM field. Courses such as GT 2303 make students aware of all the different uses of technology and science—some aspects that students might not normally be exposed to. Thus, the makerspace reinforces this idea, bringing all students to the table to discuss what they want to learn and letting them figure out the best way to do that.

Once the space was introduced, the initial reception for it was immediate and positive. From the space's inception into 2015, the library will be watching to see what happens with GT 2303. They believe it is already a success, but as time goes by, of course, they will want evaluate what is working and what is not.

MARKETING

Because so much of the Georgia Tech makerspace is taken up by GT 2303, a large percentage of its marketing is handled by the professors teaching the course. Students learn that the class will take place offering current materials in an engaging environment. As this was an experimental course and space associated with it, there has not been initially much marketing associated with the space. The plan is to develop a fuller marketing strategy after the spring 2013 semester ends after evaluating this first trial. Students were first told about the course through advisors and, as mentioned, the professors, who invited a mix of students that they thought would be a good fit for the class. Additionally, other students heard about the class from friends and wanted to be a part of this experience. Registration for the first class was full, and there is talk of opening it up to more students in the future.

The remaining time that the space is open has led to students learning about the space through word of mouth. Students tend to be drawn to open spaces in libraries, and such has been the case in this library.

Social Media

The Information Commons has its own website as well as Facebook and Twitter feeds that it uses to popularize library events and resources. These accounts are mostly dedicated to the library as a whole, but they use them to highlight events related to their makerspace. To advertise the space, the library took advantage of their social media accounts; they let their followers know about open hours and encouraged students to think of activities that they could do at the makerspace.

(This is important for libraries to take note of: you do not necessarily need a separate social media account for every department within your library. By all means, if you already have a general account, use it to promote individual events for each area of the library as needed.)

The Georgia Tech Library has a large amount of followers, and while they cannot reach the entire student body, they do have a couple hundred followers that they can easily get in contact with. It is hard to track who has seen the posts and tweets so far. Judging from usage though, slowly but surely, people are beginning to learn more about this space and seek it out.

STAFFING

The makerspace itself does not rely on a lot of people to run it. All staff in the Information Commons know about the space and are prepared to deal with any problems should they arise. The space is currently overseen by the Undergraduate Programming and Engagement Librarian (UPEL), Charlie Bennett. For the most part, Bennett deals with scheduling the room and with making sure that the space appears open and usable to walk-in patrons. He was asked at the last minute to be involved with GT 2303 so that he could be an embedded librarian in the course. He advises on projects as well as lets students know about other library resources when they are working on projects that require databases and other tools not provided in the makerspace.

(This kind of engagement serves as a model for other libraries, academic and otherwise, with staff actively collaborating with others in the makerspace. As David V. Loertscher writes, "As teacher librarians we can embrace new and innovative ideas or allow them to grow up around us, excluding us, ignoring us, or we can embrace, join, encourage, and move to the center of both serious academics and the exciting movements in disruptive education" (2012, p. 46).

The other staff and faculty within the information commons are aware of the limitations and usage rules of the makerspace, but do not get as involved with the space. The remaining faculty associated with GT 2303 comes from various backgrounds and disciplines, as reflected by their fields. They helped design the course and offered input on what they thought was needed in the makerspace. Although they did not help with the direct purchasing and organizing of the space, they were glad to have an opportunity to use the library in a unique way.

63

DEMOGRAPHICS

The library at Georgia Tech is an academic research library where the typical user of the makerspace is an undergraduate. No real differences in usage have been noted among majors at this time; of course, most of the majors at the school tend to skew toward the sciences and engineering.

One of the benefits to the course is that it is multidisciplinary, which means that course creators actively welcome students from different fields and majors, hoping to get a wide spectrum of people who bring something unique to the class. The course is open to freshmen and sophomores (the students needed a permit to enter the class), to help students become interested in new things at the start of their careers at the university, rather than at the end, when they might not have the time or money to invest into learning new things, and it might have less of an effect on them. The overall aim of the course is to help students discover innovations that can help others while also teaching students to discover the creativity within themselves.

■ ■ ■

The first priority of the Georgia Tech library makerspace is to figure out whether the course should be offered again, and if so, what they will change about how the makerspace is used in the course as well as how much time is devoted to it. Likely the most pressing issue will be evaluating the materials readily available in the makerspace and how they functioned. If a particular setup is not working, staff will need to either re-create the space or find a way to repurpose the machinery and purchase new equipment. However, with the planning that went into this makerspace, those scenarios are unlikely. If anything, the most likely changes will come from needed improvements rather than reductions or major reconsiderations.

REFERENCES

Loertscher, D. V. 2012. Maker Spaces and the Learning Commons. *Teacher Librarian*, 39, no. 6: 45–46.

National Center for Education Statistics, United States, and Institute of Education Sciences (U.S.). 2013. *Digest of Education Statistics*. Washington, D.C.: U.S. Dept. of Health, Education, and Welfare, Education Division, National Center for Education Statistics.

MESA PUBLIC LIBRARY–RED MOUNTAIN

Mesa, Arizona
www.mesalibrary.org
Public Library Branch

Mesa is the third largest city in Arizona and has a wide range of patrons for the size of their city, each with their own unique needs and skills. The city library has created four distinct branches; the Red Mountain Branch has begun the steps to create their own makerspace, and in this chapter they lay out their plan for what they expect once it is fully formed.

CREATION AND FUNDING

The funding for the makerspace—which is tied to the space's creation—has been primarily provided by the City of Mesa. Unlike with some libraries, the Mesa Public Library budget did not have enough room in it to fully fund an operational makerspace, and so they had to look around for unique funding opportunities. One of these ways involved a community-led fundraiser. This was done through a grassroots organization in the area called iMesa.

iMesa asked the citizens of the community to suggest varying ideas for what they wanted to see happen in their community. While they received many suggestions, only a few of them were able to be funded. So the iMesa program tried to find specific programs that were innovative and promoted new ideas. The makerspace program at the Mesa Public Library was one such idea that they felt was worth investing in. The program has an interesting way of determining who will receive funding and who will not. All citizens of Mesa are welcome to vote on entries, and this is seen as a way of choosing what they want their city funds to be invested in. Many of the options citizens have to invest in are public works and programs that will directly affect those that live within the city. There is a committee for the organization to offer guidance and give final approval, but they truly let anyone within the community participate and offer suggestions for what they think needs to be improved the most.

The library had initially heard about makerspaces through a slow build of reading library literature and attending conferences. The more they learned about the projects, it seemed like they would be a natural fit at their own library. So they took a look at what type of space they had available and realized that it was possible for them to build one in their own library. They put in the application with iMesa, hoping that they might be one of the projects that was funded.

iMesa was the primary funder of the program, and the library owes a great deal to them. Still, as with other libraries, Mesa Public Library has had to write grants and look for other sources of funding for some of the smaller items that could not be covered completely by iMesa. As of this writing, the library is still mid-application for some grants and waiting to hear back on the others, so they are not yet sure of their exact funding.

Fees

The library is hoping to cover all costs of the makerspace with the funds that they receive from iMesa, the grants they have applied for, and donations if possible. The library strongly feels that the space should not cost their users anything, so if they do end up placing on a fee or fine for use of the space, they anticipate it will be for the use of their 3-D printer. And this fee will likely just be a recovery fee for the weight of the digital object being printed, and nothing else extra taxed onto it. Libraries really try to embrace that attitude of keeping things free or at low cost to their patrons, believing in the spirit that everyone should have an equal opportunity to learn and use materials regardless of economic position in life.

PHYSICAL SPACE

The floor for the makerspace at the Red Mountain Branch involved taking two meeting rooms that had not been getting much use and combining them together. Although they did not have to do any construction to take over the space they did need to replan the spaces and reorganize how materials were set up in the space so that more people would have a chance to take advantage of the space and utilize it at its best capacity. The two rooms provide about 2,500 square feet that the library feels is more than adequate for their anticipated patrons. The space has glass walls and doors that create a physical barrier from the rest of the library, and they hope that this will prevent any escaping noise from polluting the rest of the library population who might not be interested in what is happening at the makerspace.

Construction

The two rooms had to have a wall knocked down so that they could be combined into one giant room, and this involved technical aspects of rerouting the air-conditioning in the space, along with some rewiring of the circuitry so that the lights and other fixtures in the room would all be connected. It was a major construction project for a small branch library. The library needed to turn the space from drab business functional meeting rooms into places that would spur creativity and make people want to stay there.

The newly renovated space received a new coat of paint. Likewise, the furniture was somewhat uninspired and purely functional for the space's former role as a meeting room. Thus there were plenty of chairs and large tables, but less spaces for building and construction. So the library had to purchase new furniture and gather things that would be conducive to creativity. Specifically, they wanted to purchase tables that would allow users to collaborate seamlessly, while also leaving room for laptops and other computers in the space.

67

TOOLS

Since the library is still in the nascent developmental plans, not all the machinery has been purchased for their space. They are looking into the commonly purchased and used items in makerspaces, but some of the items that they think would be best suited to their needs would be new Mac and PC computers. They stress that they want to have a representative sampling of each type, so that users can have a choice between what they use as well as what they can learn on. Other equipment that they are considering is a sewing machine. The library believes that this type of handcrafting of projects will encourage their users to learn accessible projects among things that they can likely do at home, but wouldn't have considered.

Although they cannot yet give numbers as to how many people are using the space and at what times, they have purposely built the space so that it doesn't center solely on their programming. They want the space to be in use at all times, not just when one of the staff members happens to be leading a program. They plan on having an open door policy so that patrons can feel free to walk in and make use of the space on their own, regardless of whether or not there is someone waiting inside to give them guided direction.

PROGRAMMING

While creativity and innovation is going to be a strong focus of the makerspace, the Mesa Public Library has also chosen to turn their space into a collaborative workspace. Their programs will have the aim of improving the lives of their members that is in part driven by the choices of their own patrons. They don't want to dictate to their patrons about what they can and cannot do in the space, so if there is a strong demand for one type of program over another, the library is willing to work with those demands. It is an admirable flexibility that encourages users to come to the classes that they have helped design and create. At the moment they are planning on creating classes that teach and utilize the following skill sets: robotics programs, video recording programs, crafts, sewing, coding, CAD, 3-D design, photo editing, creative writing, best practices in business, marketing, retirement help, college planning, and more when they get full feedback from their users.

They have a strong will to create programs that will teach their patrons how to create from every level of the design process. Especially through teaching CAD, they know that many of the designs that are eventually created with 3-D printers are created with CAD or other similar programs. They do alert patrons to the existence of Thingiverse (a site with free files to create 3-D-printed objects) in case a patron does not want to use CAD to create her own file. They feel that by allowing their patrons to have an input in every step of the design process that patrons will not only learn more, but will come to appreciate their project much more because they created it completely themselves and did not have to rely on the help of others.

Sectioning

Each of the space's programs will be aimed at unique population sets. This range will go from kids and teens to 19- to 30-year-olds, and 31- to 50-year-olds, as well as 50-plus, if they can get enough interest . While everyone is welcome to attend the sessions, they do want to keep everyone in roughly the same age groups. With the exception of parents in the kids groups, they really want to encourage everyone to be able to work at their own level. The library feels that if they have too mixed of an age group, the classes will not work as well; they feel that certain groups would work faster than others, which would cause the slower participants to feel inadequate and the faster participants to feel bored and not wish to participate in future activities. Moderating the pacing of these classes is key, and so they have chosen to break the classes up into different age ranges so that they can better accommodate the paces of their patrons. Although they have a fair idea of how they want to break their age groups apart, if they find that the older groups of 19 to 30, 30 to 50, and 50+ are not working quite as well as they had hoped, they are willing to rework the pairings so that they start getting more appropriate age levels paired together.

Along this vein, there will be some classes offered to unique population sets. This is done for a few reasons, but staff likely will not be teaching the business classes to their kid and teen populations, just because they do not feel it will be relevant to the needs of those users. Some of the more hands-on activities will be aimed at only the younger patrons; the library wants to have activities that will teach these patrons fine motor skills along with certain other skills that, while fun, might not hold the attention of one of their older patrons.

The overall goal is to have patrons engaged and interested in the activities offered, so staff are trying their best to make sure that no matter what they implement, each patron leaves the activities feeling like they have learned something and that they enjoyed themselves. It is very much a work in progress, so the library is trying to figure out what works best for each group.

69

MARKETING

One of the marketing blessings in disguise for the library has been the construction of the new space. It was unexpected, but as the library began work on the space with lots of noise, dust and new people in the library moving about their patrons began to ask questions about what was going on in the space: "What is the noise about?" and "What are you building?" As the staff answered these questions, their patrons became more and more interested in the space, eager to try it out for themselves once the construction was over with.

In addition to relying on the natural curiosity of their patrons, the library has placed signs near the space letting people know about what it will become, although hours and availability have not yet been posted. This is in part because they are still exploring their options to figure out what they want the hours to be. Because the space is not operational as of this writing, they do not know how many people to expect using the space. They have tried to lay out some preparatory models so that they can have an idea for when they are scheduling and marketing their events and classes.

Later, as the space has more definite plans that they can firmly announce to their patrons, the library plans to utilize more traditional marketing methods, such as to place signs by the entrance and to create summer programming that the library can count on children and parents attending during the summer break. Likely these events will also be posted on their website calendar and other forms of communication with the community, such as their social media platforms. With these methods combined, they have tried to build a steady sense of excitement for the opening of the makerspace.

Social Media

Like many other libraries addressed here, social media has offered the library a rich chance to speak to their patrons without investing much capital. The library uses Twitter (@MesaLibrary) to speak to its users. It should be noted that the Twitter account is used to communicate news about all branches of the library, and not just the Red Mountain Branch. For the most part this is fine, but this means that they do not have a dedicated account for just their makerspace. Thus, they plan to announce events and activities as they take place, making sure to specify the location on their account so that they can avoid potential confusion. Library systems with multiple branches often have to deal with patrons going to the wrong branch when trying to attend specific events. There is not a lot the library can do to prevent this, but they do try to make sure that their users are aware of which branch the makerspace will be housed at. Their Facebook account is dedicated to their teen services, and so reaches only a small subset of potential users. Still, the library aims to alert those teen users to appropriate programs when the time comes. This is all part of their multifronted plan to reach users in any manner possible.

STAFFING

The THINKspot Coordinator is the primary person in charge of operating the makerspace, but the plan is to have help from community volunteers on an as-needed basis, as well as to get help from other staff members when the space has a very busy schedule. Staff are even open to getting interns from the local community college library science program. They are still trying to figure out how many volunteers and aides they will need for each individual program, because they believe that some will require more hands-on direction. These choices will be made as lesson plans are built and other details are finalized.

In the Anchorage Public Library profile, the concept of a maker-in-residence was discussed. Although the Mesa Public Library briefly considered this option, they felt that it was not the right choice for them at that time; one consideration was that they felt a maker-in-residence would impede on their collaborative learning environment. They did not want the lessons to be handed down by one person; they wanted the makerspace to be a project that everyone could feel comfortable adding to or changing parts of. Although the coordinator is working as a one-woman operation for much of the makerspace, she is not the maker-in-residence.

The library also decided against a maker-in-residence because their library was already operating on a small budget; the cost of hiring a maker in addition to a coordinator was out of the question. In the future, if more funds are secured, this might be something that they are willing to consider.

DEMOGRAPHICS

The core users at the Mesa Public Library tend to be older and retired patrons, along with a heavier set of teenagers and children during summer vacations, with parents usually accompanying the smaller children. Because the room is not yet fully open, it is hard to gauge what the public's reaction will be to the room, but staff have watched as more and more people peer into the windows and try to guess what is going on inside the space. Though they did not intentionally try to create an air of mystique surrounding the space, they have found that this added benefit certainly is not hurting demand to use the space. They are anticipating that use of the space will take on the effect of a slow build, with more and more patrons slowly coming to take advantage of the space—especially during the summer, when they expect to have more teenagers and children in the building.

Forms

As to whether they will implement a permission form, the library is still considering its options. They will likely implement one depending on the types of people they think could be exposed to harm or if they are advised to by their counsel.

Some of the bigger libraries tend to keep lawyers on retainer for specific legal issues that they might have from time to time. If your library happens to take the advice of a lawyer, it might be worth discussing with them about how you would like to draft your permission slips and liability forms. Although the language in these forms can often seem a bit dense and archaic, it can help all parties out should the form be needed for any reason. Some libraries have forms regarding potential injury, while others have forms that discuss the use of photos and videos on the internet and other publications.

Creating these forms really depends on the internal policies of your own library. Rarely are they created in order to cause extra headaches and paperwork for all involved. They are designed to protect the users and to make things smoother down the line for everyone involved. So while the Mesa Public Library already has a few forms in place for their other programs, they are in the process of deciding what will be best for their own makerspace and whether a permission slip is truly needed for use of the space.

■ ■ ■

While the Mesa Public Library Red Mountain Branch is still waiting for grants and trying to figure out what they want to do with their space, they have already laid the foundation for an excellent makerspace. Some of the things that they have done which any library could do is to research what other libraries are doing, as well as to invest in some core pieces of machinery. They looked at the needs of the patrons and were sure to purchase only the things that would directly help out their patrons, and then they found the opportunities that would let them bring these things to their patrons. This was through applying for grants and looking for every extra option they could find. This required persistence and research skill, but it was certainly a task that the library was up for.

Because they do not have any real-world examples to build on, the library is currently trying to guess when the peak times for use of the space will be. In part, they are trying to figure out when they can schedule programs to receive the maximum participants, but they also want to know when they should make their operating hours for the space. Most libraries express that no time works perfectly with everyone; even when a library thinks that they have finally found the perfect time, they will have no-shows and people who cannot stay for the entire duration. Learning how to deal with these aspects of scheduling can be trying, but if you can figure out the basics of what your patrons want with regard to open times, then you can at least please some of the people, some of the time.

If your library is considering building or repurposing a space to become a makerspace, follow the example of the Mesa Public Library. Look at the resources available to you, think creatively about finding funding, and consider what is most important for your space to offer to your patrons. A patron-driven makerspace will ultimately be successful because it offers to the public what they had always been asking for. It is impossible to please everyone, but it is worthwhile trying to attempt to please most of them.

MICHIGAN MAKERS GROUP

Plymouth, MI
http://michiganmakers.weebly.com/
School Library

In Plymouth, Michigan a distinctive afterschool program is taking place in the East Middle School where students are participating in a makerspace environment. Unlike many makerspaces, the Michigan Makers group is a unique and interesting joint venture between University of Michigan LIS students and local middle schools to create an afterschool program that teaches young children about makerspaces and the maker movement.

Many of the makerspaces highlighted in this book occur in academic or public library environments, but it is important to point out that these makerspaces are the type of spaces that would thrive with a school-age population. Indeed many public makerspaces aim theirs at school-age children. Below are the details of how the makerspace was arranged in a school environment.

CREATION

Sometimes with makerspaces librarians can be worried that these spaces will not be accepted or well understood by their populace before they are fully implemented. This can be a valid concern in some situations, but luckily, this was not the case at the East Middle School. In many ways the idea for the makerspace came from the students themselves. The librarian at East, Rachel Goldberg, was teaching an education technology unit one day that had students playing the ALICE programming module. The students were immediately fascinated by the technology.

Realizing that this unit was having an unusual effect on her students—they were even coming in during their lunch hour to play with the technology—Goldberg began to teach herself a few more programming languages and tools, and kept holding more and more tutorials for the students who were so fascinated by these new technologies. This was a great leap for the students, but even though their own programming skills were soaring, it was obvious that this was only a stopgap that could not last for much longer.

Goldberg began to think of her options for how to help these students keep learning while making sure that they were not skipping lunch and had time to do their own school work. Eventually she stumbled on the idea of working with the local iSchool at the University of Michigan. From there she began to make contacts with interested faculty and graduate students, specifically Kristin Fontichiaro, who coordinates the school library media program at the University of Michigan.

On the side of the iSchool, they saw this as an excellent opportunity to get involved with local school libraries and also to experiment with the new ideas they had been hearing about makerspaces. Everyone saw this as a unique opportunity to give students a place to explore their interests. Prior to turning this into an organized setting for the students, it was becoming unsustainable, because the librarian just simply could not keep up with the demands of her students. With the added help of the graduate students and the faculty member at UM's iSchool, they were able to make it structured without stripping the original purpose behind why they were teaching the kids.

The program had the unique opportunity to ask for and accept students as if it were a course enrollment. The pilot program was designed to have only twenty students attending the program, but due to the high demand they had to double this to forty and eventually had to turn away an additional ten students. So the program has definitely not suffered from a lack of interest; if anything, the program has thoroughly blossomed.

FUNDING

Funding for the Michigan Makers group came from a variety of sources, but their chief source of income came from a small $1,400 grant from the Michigan Association for Computer Users in Education, approximately $300 from a faculty member at the University of Michigan's research fund, and a generous donation for a 3-D printer (which typically can be very expensive).

Fees

The group intentionally chose not to implement a fee for use of the space. They want to make this a highly accessible space for children, and they do not want to purposely cull out those students who cannot afford the fee, feeling that these students are the ones most likely to need the space anyway.

PHYSICAL SPACE

Although the Michigan Makers group involves the pairing of two independent groups, the actual activities take place in the school library of East Middle School based in in Plymouth, Michigan. The program takes place one day a week after school has been let out.

The makerspace is physically based in the school library of East Middle School. Since the makerspace activities happen after school and students are allowed to have free range of the entire library, the school has not had to do any renovations or remodeling of the space. This is in part because most of their machinery is small enough to be stored in cabinets, and also reliant on the fact that noise levels are not a major concern for them. Very few other after school programs are taking place during this time, so the students have license to be as loud as they need to be to complete their project. Occasionally the staff might need to rearrange some furniture if they are working on a particularly complex project, but it is all things that can be quickly put back in place ready for the next morning.

TOOLS

Choosing the right materials for the space involved careful thought into how young children would be using these materials. The Michigan Makers group intentionally chose inexpensive or cheap materials because they wanted their students to really feel free to play with and tinker with their tools. They did not want students to be hindered by fear of breaking an item. They wanted tools that could be easily replaced if they were broken, yet capable of withstanding a good deal of abuse. This was for both the relief of students and program administrators. They reasoned that there was no purpose in having a device that everyone was afraid to use, because it was too special or difficult to use. With those use and purchasing parameters in their head, the core machines that they ended up purchasing were basic computers for HTML, photo manipulation, and Scratch. They also purchased Arduinos, Squishy Circuits (these consist of dough, batteries, battery packs, LEDs, etc.), miscellaneous crafting supplies such as craft paper, markers, poster board, vinyl, construction paper, scissors, and glue. They also have recently purchased a 3-D printer and Raspberry Pi microcomputers that they will be introducing to the school shortly. The Raspberry Pi computers are fully functioning Linux based computers that can be purchased for only $35. The program was immediately intrigued by their price tag and by the functions that they said they could do. Ellen Gustafson said about finding cheap resources for the space, "From the beginning of our planning, we had a kind of sixth sense that we might be creating something that members of our team would want to be able to replicate on a minimal budget after graduation, when they got jobs in various kinds of libraries and informal learning environments."

Although the space itself is fairly large and they can host a good number of students, their ideal plan, guided by the school librarian, was to have students working together in small groups. Ideally this would mean only having two or three children working together at one station. Part of the reasoning for this was based on a desire for the space to have a strong collaborative component. They did not want the space to be a place for students to work individually in silence. Rather they wanted the young students to learn how to work together and develop not only STEM skills, but also basic communication skills that would help them learn to partner together and communicate their needs and desires effectively.

PROGRAMMING

The programs at the East Middle School makerspace follow a certain pattern that gives predictability to their students who appreciate routine and rhythm. Each session begins with one of the teachers taking attendance. Then a mentor will explain each of the activity options for the day. For the most part, they try not to overload the students with options, so each week they offer two technology related options and one craft. They discovered that some students like the instant gratification of creating something tangible and with immediacy over other projects that could take a great deal of time to see the end product.

Their working theory is that they need to offer these varying options because their school-age makerspace differs wildly from makerspaces aimed at adults. With adult makerspaces, an adult might join to learn about an already identified hobby. Adults also have the luxury of being able to drop in and choose the specific skill set they want to learn, whereas this afterschool program requires that the students attend. Students do not get as much choice about whether they are there or not, so staff wanted to give the students an opportunity to at least choose what they were doing while they attended the maker program. Students also always have the option of working on their own projects if they do not like any of the weekly offerings. For example, one craft introduced to students was origami. Offered piles of colored paper and several detailed instructions, the students spent their time carefully folding and trying to recreate paper cranes, tortoises, and other paper fauna. An added benefit to this model is that it allows each child to work at their own pace and skill level.

The parents of the students at East Middle School have also gotten involved in the project. While not all the parents have the capability or the time to drop by and help, the father of one of the students was familiar with some of the materials, and often came by to help set up the machinery, such as the Raspberry Pis. He even organized a field trip to Dearborn, Michigan, to visit the tech lab and have circuit boards cut using lasers for the students. He filmed video of this, and the students who were not able to make the trip with him were able to watch how their circuit boards that they assembled themselves were carved and created. It was a great way to allow the students to see everything from literal start to finish. Letting the students work on these circuit boards also allows for them to have hands on learning and see how each individual connection is made.

There is a big emphasis at the Michigan Makers group on understanding each level of detail so that you can understand the whole. They do not try to present things to their students as a giant unit, but rather to break things into understandable parts. This approach is not overwhelming to the students, and they have greatly appreciated having the hands-on experience of learning it as they build it themselves. It gives them a great sense of accomplishment as they create something that they can actually use themselves.

Group Work and Supervision

The graduate students are split up into groups in relation to the different projects going on that day, so that each module will have mentors associated with it, who will know the background and tasks to do for it. These mentors will demonstrate the project for the students so that they can understand the tools and key concepts associated with the project. After that they leave some time for questioning, and just let the students have at it and figure out the projects on their own.

One of the ideas that they made sure to incorporate into the program was to always leave the last fifteen minutes for students to write about their experiences in their maker journals. These are just simple journals that they have the students use to discuss their work and what they are excited about in it. This brings a writing element into the curriculum that prepares them for the future when they might write lab reports or other technical writing. Sometimes the topics take more than one session to be fully explored, so they purposely build in time to deal with projects thoroughly.

Although most of the grad students who participate in the program are based in Ann Arbor, Plymouth is only a short twenty-minute drive from campus. Occasionally the grad students can't attend due to things such as exams and other iSchool responsibilities. On these days, the students are allowed to revisit past projects and work on their own private projects that require less supervision.

There is a strong move to create independence among the students attending this program. Staff want students to learn how to think about STEM skills and creativity, but beyond this, they also want to build a real sense of leadership within these kids. They stress to the students that anyone can be a student, just as anyone can be a teacher. With these lines drawn, they make sure to show that the mentors and adults of the program can just as easily learn from their students. For example, one of the programs that has gone over very well among their students is teaching them the idea of how to pitch a concept. Teachers stress to students the idea of how to back up work with facts and sell an idea or concept to others with facts.

Rachel Goldberg wrote about some of their initial troubles with starting up the makerspace in a short article for YALSA, saying, "We've run into some small obstacles with filters and software that prevents downloads, but all these experiences have provided us with opportunities to have meaningful conversations with students about Internet filters, responsible online behavior, and, in some cases, the mechanics of hardware, software, and the way that downloads or websites are actually blocked" (Goldberg, 2013). The staff at the Michigan Makers group has a unique way of taking potential problems such as filter obstacles and turning them into new ways to learn. Students can be naturally curious about not just why content might be filtered from them, but this leads to specific questions about how filtering works, and learning the basics of these things that they encounter in their everyday life.

Crafting

Often the ideas of traditional library outreach services, such as knitting club or story time, can get mixed up with the idea of makerspaces. After all, makerspaces certainly seem to do many of the same things, just with an engineering bent. They both have interactive elements, but one of the main differences with a makerspace is that you are engaging a new type of patron at the library. This type is someone who has a very directed approach to learning, and who does not want a book tie-in to the activity; these are people who are more technology focused.

One program that the Michigan Makers have employed that fuses the traditional with the modern activity is when they brought in sewing machines for their students to work with. It was a hit in part because the class spent a lot of the time focusing on how sewing machines work. The students watched a brief video that demonstrated what the needle and thread were doing in the machines, displaying how stitches were made. Then students partnered up using the buddy system, as the mentors were accounting for any accidental injuries that might occur with young students using sewing machines. The first sewing project was to make a pillow. Students were given free rein in how they designed their pillows, but they were to incorporated a few basic elements, such as a straight line, a curve, and an angle. With such parameters in place, students explored on their own how the machines worked. The project provided structure and guidelines to work within without being highly prescriptive.

MARKETING

Because the program is based in a school library, the marketing for the makerspace was slightly different than the type of marketing that could be expected for a typical public or academic library. The library is working with a specific population set, and they did not want to expand beyond that. The total population of the entire school is only 760 kids, so they had to keep their expectations based around those numbers. They wanted to stick solely with the students at East Middle School. They were open to all age ranges within the school population.

Marketing options the library considered were making morning announcements over the PA system, advertising in the school newsletter, or sending e-mails directly to parents to encourage them to enroll their children in the program. Instead, what they opted to do was post information on the school website as well as signs throughout the school hallways. This relatively simple campaign created excitement for the program. They asked simple questions such as "Does the idea of turning play dough into an electrical circuit make you light up?" "Have you ever looked inside a computer?" and "Want to make clothing out of duct tape?" Each of these questions appeared on posters on hallways, followed by the simple directive to show up at the next related afterschool program to find out more.

The ads did a good job of drumming up excitement and an air of mystery, which created a small word of mouth environment. Students wanted to know the answers to these questions, and while the library initially began the project with just a handful of students, they ended up having to cap attendance because they had too many students wanting to participate. This was their best-case scenario, and in this instance the marketing for it worked extremely well. They received more students than they had anticipated.

Staff plan to resume marketing with posters and e-mails, as they expect some students to graduate from the program and move on to high school; they also want to remind students who may have forgotten about the program over the summer break.

STAFFING

With the number of students limited to just forty students, the designers of the makerspace intentionally wanted to make sure that there was a high ratio of teachers or mentors to students. They wanted students to have access to as much guidance as possible, rather than having one or two librarians stretched thin trying to reach out to the entire group.

The middle school librarian guides the program, along with eight graduate students and a graduate school professor from the University of Michigan School of Information. In addition to these regular staff members, three ninth-grade "alumni" of the program come back to help facilitate events as their schedule allows. Between the ten regular staff members of the makerspace and the three ninth-graders, program staff feel they have an excellent ratio of students to teachers. The overall mission of the crew is both to teach mini lessons on various skills each week and to monitor the progress of the students and offer aid when needed. Staff participate in the activities alongside their students, helping them with steps that might be more difficult, or simply helping with small tasks, such as locating an item.

Although 2013 was the first year that the program has been up and running, the plan is to make this a continuing partnership between the middle school and the university, as there will be a continuing amount of graduate students who want to be school librarians or children's librarians. (Graduate students stay for an average of two years.) In 2013, about half of the student mentors are graduating, with the other half planning on returning in the fall. It will likely continue in this manner for the length of the program.

DEMOGRAPHICS

The typical student at East Middle School comes from a suburban environment. During the school day, the students come to the library periodically in their classes to use the computers, conduct research, and check out books. This is usually on a schedule class basis, similar to many information literacy classes that academic librarians may be used to teaching. However, during the lunch period, the library acts as a space for the students to go to pursue their own interests, as well as hosting various book groups, and where other clubs gather to meet. It can be a very busy space depending on the day and time. With those schedule conflicts in mind, a stable time was set for the Michigan Makers group for every Tuesday after school from 3:00 to 4:30 pm. During these ninety minutes, students would have the opportunity to learn the project for the week, as well as to develop their own ideas and build their own projects based off of the model. The timing is also ideal, because it allows for everyone to have plenty of time to address their individual needs, rather than rushing and trying to fit everything into the space of one hour.

Staff did not try to distinguish what type of age groups that they wanted from the school. Since they have a rather small population to begin with of only grades 6 to 8, they welcomed everyone from those grades, figuring that most of them would be functioning and working on about the same levels. For those that were more advanced or a little behind the others, aides would come in, who could help the slower students catch up and offer the quicker ones individual attention to work on smaller projects.

In the end, the program filled up incredibly quickly, and they did not need to worry about whether or not they would be able to get enough students to fill the program. They do not know if this was based on their marketing efforts or if the group would have just naturally filled up on its own. There was already a small computer club going that could have helped build the momentum, but the club was not near the size that the makers group ended up being.

Forms

Since this makerspace is based in a middle-school environment with children who are under 18, permission forms signed by parents or guardians was a given. It was never an option for the designers of this program to even consider not offering permission slips. In order for any student to use the machines and participate in a meaningful way at the library makerspace, they had to have a permission slip turned in. Once the form was submitted, the students were given license to take part in everything at the makerspace.

■ ■ ■

Because this makerspace sprang naturally from the ideas of the students, its success seems natural too. The Michigan Makers program took the approach of seizing on what the needs of their patrons were. They had students who were clamoring to know more about programming, but the administration realized that they did not have the capacity to handle that. They sought out the resources that would help these students, and in the end found a project that would continue for years to come, and became well loved by even those outside of the original core group.

REFERENCE

Goldberg, Rachel. 2013. "Michigan Makers (Winter 2013)." *Young Adult Library Services* 11, no. 2 (March 19, 2013). www.yalsa.ala.org/yals/michigan-makers-winter-2013/.

URBANA FREE LIBRARY

Urbana, IL
http://urbanafreelibrary.org/
Medium-Sized Public Library

Based in Central Illinois, Urbana is a small city of about forty thousand people. The city houses most of the campus of University of Illinois at Urbana-Champaign, which also has a huge student population that mirrors the towns own population. The university has a Graduate School of Library and Information Science, GSLIS, which has also helped the library in a few of its projects from time to time.

The Urbana Free Library has many distinguishing characteristics; in particular, it was established in 1874, which makes it one of the first public libraries to be established in the state of Illinois. The current version of the library has changed a great deal since those early days, particularly in the areas of their makerspace that they are doing innovative work with.

CREATION

The makerspace at Urbana is primarily geared towards teenage users, though other ages are certainly welcome to take part in using the space when classes are not being taught. The plan is to initially test out ideas for running the makerspace on the teen users, and then eventually to roll out classes and models of instruction for other adult populations and groups that are using the library.

When the Urbana Free Library was first designing the lab and trying to think of how to program their space, they looked at other makerspace programs across the country. They eventually struck onto YOUmedia at the Chicago Public Library. They had heard good things about the program and were impressed by the ideas that they saw coming from there. So they decided to loosely model their makerspace on many of the core structures and concepts found at YOUmedia.

One of the core concepts that the library thought was important to stress was for teens to be able to approach technology on their own terms. The library tried to avoid prescriptive programs about how to do something and instead see the space as a mashup of a DIY facility with many tools alongside a media production space giving users the freedom to explore their own creativity. When the teens have the freedom to explore without explicit directives, they end up using the space in ways that the staff at Urbana had not previously imagined.

FUNDING

Most of the funding for the Urbana programs has come from library funding directly, but many of their gadgets were purchased through a grant that they received from the Department of Commerce and Economic Opportunity in the State of Illinois. Since this project is a hybrid media production area and a makerspace, the library was able to get more funding for this unique type of programming.

Fees

Realizing that their patrons come from a wide range of backgrounds, and in keeping with the general mission of their library, the Urbana Free Library has not imposed a fee to use or create materials in the makerspace. The library does everything it can to keep the costs of use to the library itself and not passed along onto their patrons. They do not want a fee—no matter how seemingly nominal—to limit someone from participating in the activities and lessons that they offer. They feel that it is something vital to offer to the community, and a fee should not stop anyone from having access to it.

This is typical of many of the libraries interviewed in this process. The libraries that charge for the use of a makerspace are rarely, if ever, trying to turn a profit on their space. It is seen as more a way to recoup the costs of some of the more costly materials that are used in the creation and design of the activities there. As mentioned in "About Makerspaces: Concerns and Considerations," most such charges are for filament, something these libraries compare to charge for paper at a printer; 3-D printers, they rationalize, are just fancier versions of regular copiers and printers, which users are already accustomed to having to pay a fee for.

PHYSICAL SPACE

Before the makerspace at Urbana Free Library could even get set up, there were debates about where to place it. A renovation had taken place at the library seven years before, but despite this, there was not currently any free space for them to settle on, and another renovation was out of the question.

The way they eventually settled on a location was twofold: first, they partnered with a local middle school afterschool program to bring their programming to, turning the makerspace into a mobile lab that could be brought to the students wherever they were. Still, they wanted a more permanent space as well. They decided to use their library auditorium, which is on the ground level and covers a 26-by-48-foot space. The spacious room is not in use all the time, and it allows for patrons to have room to explore and work together when it is scheduled for their makerspace, though it is often used for other library projects as well.

With a space as large as the auditorium, the fire code allows for up to eighty people in the room at any given time. The programs were initially designed for only ten to thirty people, because they wanted it to have an intimate air, an easy level of manageability for the instructors. Now that the program has begun to excel and build buzz, the library is looking into new ways to expand the number of participants, realizing that many more people are interested in it than they had initially hoped for. (The planning for only a small handful of patrons had been based on their estimation of interest and how many instructors and staff members they had available to them to work in the makerspace at any given time.)

Noise Issues

The library is very aware that this makeshift use of space has created some problems with noise. The space shares a wall with the children's department, and while users try to remain conscious of the noise they create in the space, they realize that sometimes it is impossible to keep the volume in check. Particularly because this space is devoted to teenagers, patrons often have to be reminded to keep the noise levels down. (It is less an issue of the machinery creating too much noise, and more of an issue of the excitability of the patrons.) In a sense, this noise is a good thing, but it is something that the library tries to remain aware of and keep from getting out of hand. They want to be sensitive to the needs of their other patrons, many of whom come for a quiet space to study.

TOOLS

A majority of the funding for the Urbana makerspace came from a variety of grants, and for that reason some of their equipment options were limited by their funding institutions. They have a UP! 3-D printer and a silhouette Cameo vinyl cutter. Their mini lab that they take to the middle schools and use as a mobile makerspace carries a charging cart, a mobile access point, a shared external drive, a color printer, a document camera, a projector, video cameras, and seven laptops. Currently staff are in developmental talks with their community Informatics Club to receive an additional ten laptops that they hope they can use for 3-D design on the mobile mini lab. They requested these extra laptops because they soon realized that their initial seven laptops were getting so much use and were in such high demand that they needed many more than they had originally anticipated. Every library dreams of having good problems like these—so much demand for their program that they just cannot keep up—but when staff were faced with this challenge, they had to think on their feet and look to their supporters to find places to get help.

PROGRAMMING

Because they have two different types of makerspaces currently running in their library—the mobile mini lab at the middle schools and the more permanent, physical one in the library auditorium—Urbana Free Library has found that they need to create unique types of programming for each version of the makerspace. Though the versions have similar features, not all the same projects can be done at both places. This is in part due to space considerations, but also because of the types of equipment that they can carry with them to other areas outside of the library.

Their middle school programming is called "Splash," hosted every Wednesday at an afterschool program for about twenty teens. They have made the afterschool program open to all teens and do not set restrictions on who can use it or what they can do; they just want the program available for anyone who is interested to participate.

One of their other types of programming revolves around what they have dubbed as their Tufl Tech Series (*Tufl* stands for "The Urbana Free Library"). These run seasonally, with classes available each Wednesday and Thursday, featuring open one-hour labs where anyone was welcome to walk in and participate without signing up prior to the event. These were held during the afternoons—when, staff reasoned, the teens were most likely to be out of school, but before they had to go home or be at other afterschool events. This program culminated at the end of the March for their Teen Tech Week, which encouraged teen users to take advantage of all the various technologies available from the FabLabs and makers program. This functioned as a wrap-up project to celebrate the work the teens had put in while also encouraging new teens to come see what the programs had to offer. Even if the regular sessions were no longer offered, the tools would still be available to patrons.

Targeting Teens

In contrast to programming where they have invited all ages of teens from different areas of the city to attend their afterschool program, the library has taken a different approach to their regular sessions in the actual institution. Thursdays are devoted to a core group of teenagers who are more familiar with the library space. This core group of older teens acts as peer mentors to younger teens by showcasing the benefits of using the makerspace, while at the same time allowing for the younger teens to learn at their own pace. The library's reasoning behind this programming is multifold. They want to bring together disparate populations of teens—groups who would not normally meet up for various reasons, be that location, economic status, age, or any other reason. The library wanted to create a peer mentoring program that would be built via word of mouth. The plan was that on Thursdays, the core group of teens would come into the makerspace for the general program, which would be staffed by volunteers. Then over the following week, that core group would get excited about what was available to them and return to the Wednesday sessions to mentor the middle school program, to finish whatever project they happened to be working on as well as spreading the word about the Thursday program.

The core group of students is an older population, mostly juniors and seniors in high school. The staff at the library have realized that many of the younger children, particularly the middle school students, look up to and watch the older students. Staff think that perhaps if the younger middle school students see the older core group going to the afterschool program or hear them talking about the makerspace, those younger students may be inclined to join the older high school students. This is a small idea the library had about trying to get younger students interested by having the older students model what works for them. The library came up with this model based on other programs the library had previously and successfully implemented.

Another reasoning behind the peer mentoring is that staff found it was useful to foster partnerships if they had separate events for each the FabLab and the Makers program, believing that when everything is combined, it becomes harder to delineate whose task is whose; when they created different times for each program

87

to meet, the two programs could explore what worked and what did not work for each. Although the space is only open twice a week as of this writing, the library considers this a test run and hopes to expand the makerspace hours once they have figured out how much demand for the space there will actually be. They also have to factor in that they are taking up space in the auditorium, so they will not always have first priority to the space if someone else wants to book the room for a special event. This has not been a major issue for them yet though.

Gaming and Other Technology

Some of the specific programs that the Urbana makers have created revolve around using Spore and the Up printer for teens to create their own monsters. For those not familiar with Spore, it is a computer game produced by Electronic Arts that has users create thousands of variations of creatures and monsters who roam and play on an Earth-like planet. The game allows for a lot of user-generated content, and the library felt that the gaming portion would be well received by their students. Other projects that they have had the teens use at the makerspace involved having their teens create stop-motion movies using their digital cameras and other tools. These were short films that each student created, learning how they could create motion just by making tiny movements using various artistic mediums and photographing each change of position. They have also used several Arduino kits to teach their teens how to do synthesizer building. Each of the programs has met with varying degrees of success, but the library is eager to add more programs to the roster so that they can get even more folks involved.

MARKETING

Marketing for the Urbana Free Library has had to involve mostly small projects and a few direct demonstrations so that people would begin to be aware of what is available to them. The library was lucky to have a graphics department that kindly designed posters for the library and printed them up on 8.5-by-11-foot tabletop acrylic sheets. These posters were placed across the library in key areas where teens were likely to take notice of them—mostly in the already developed teen areas, as well as on display boards near the front entrances.

One unique thing the library thought to do with their marketing was to bring their 3-D printer into a public space rather than to keep it locked away in a secure staff area. It sits at the reference desk, where many people at once can see it functioning and operating. Patrons generally gather round to watch the 3-D printer work and ask questions about what it's doing and who could use it. This subtle method of marketing helped spread the word about the makerspace without the library having to spend extra money. They could take what equipment they already had and just bring it to the attention of their users without dominating the scene or conversation. People who were interested would naturally be drawn to the machine, but to those people who were not interested in the printer don't have to be assaulted by loud or intrusive advertising. This very subtle form of marketing has worked very well. So far they have noticed that whenever they run the 3-D printer, they get curious onlookers who want to know what's going on. There was some mild debate about which desks should house the printer, but eventually the settled on the reference desk based on space available and the visibility factor.

For libraries looking for a cheap way to market their events, this is certainly one method worth taking a look at. Staff have made the best of what they have and still managed to get people talking about it without actively forcing them to pay attention.

89

Social Media

Social media has also played a huge role for the Urbana library. Joel Spencer, the adult services/teen librarian, has been in charge of tweeting and blogging for the library, and he has used a majority of these platforms to alert their followers to specific events that have taken place or will be taking place in order to drum up support and visitors. Their Twitter account (@UrbanaLibrary) has over one thousand followers, whom they try to tweet to and reach around once or twice a day. They try to create a tone of excitement about the events happening at the library and express that to their followers. They have promoted articles about how their various programs have been praised throughout their local network, and they take efforts to make sure that the programs they are trying to get people to attend are very well received generally.

On their Facebook page, they have nearly two thousand likes—nearly double the amount of followers they have Twitter. This number is fairly representative of most library social media accounts, with more followers on Facebook than Twitter. On their timeline, they make sure to post lots of photos of events at the library as well as to highlight what types of events they have going on at the FabLab and Makerspace.

STAFFING

The FabLab and Maker program would be unable to run if not for the efforts of the many eager and helpful volunteers. The library is lucky to have many volunteers; the list of just technology volunteers is impressively long, with over fifty volunteers throughout the year serving to help the library with various issues in setting up and running their maker programs. The library also has student volunteers from GSLIS and other teachers from the community. Some libraries wish they could get numbers of volunteers that high for their entire library, but here they are lucky that they can get so many volunteers devoted just to their programs. They have a select group of individuals that they can rely upon, and it has been a great pool for them to work with, allowing them to attract more users to come and take advantage of the opportunities brought by these volunteers and staff members.

About two people working with teen groups in particular. There is a volunteer from their FabLab as well as their community ambassador. The community ambassador was a position that the library created to help the library identify the varied technology needs of the underserved populations in their community network. They feel it is important to have at least two people there at any given time. While the program can be run with just one person, the library thinks it is easier for two people to help run the program. So while one may be teaching and laying out the plan, another can be walking around the room and offering guidance to those who might be confused on smaller aspects of the lesson.

Joel Spencer has helped to set up the makerspace from the start. He led the redesign of the project and has been its chief promoter, helping think of new ideas to bring to the program and finding new ways to get more people involved in the space. This has involved knowing who in the community to contact, as well as knowing where to go to find out what types of technology will be needed in a growing makerspace program. The program has relied on the contacts of all the librarians at GSLIS, as well as on exposure to other makerspaces that they've seen and read about. As a combination adult services/teen services librarian, Spencer hopes to bridge these two worlds with the makers program so that both can equally participate in the project. Spencer also has a background in building and construction, so he was able to take those skills and apply them here in unique ways.

DEMOGRAPHICS

The Urbana Free Public library has no typical patron that they can reliably predict will come in. With that disclaimer, they have a healthy population of teen patrons who regularly use the library, as well as children, the elderly, and a large university student base. The area has a relatively high poverty rate and suffers from a lack of social services; due in part to this, the library sees a larger number of homeless, jobless, and mentally ill patrons. They try to serve each of their unique patron types as best they can.

COMMUNITY REACTION

Although it is still very early in the development of the Urbana makers program, they have had a generally positive reaction to the coming of the makerspace. There were several people who commented on the 3-D printer, discussing the projects they wanted to create but had not previously known they could do at the library. Early on, staff were approached by a botanist from the community who wanted to create 3-D models of pollen to use for education purposes in his classes; he was eager to learn how to use the printer to create these models. Another community member, a potter, was watching the 3-D printer work and came up with the idea to print out block text that he could imprint into his work before firing it. The staff have observed that just having people watch the printer seems to inspire certain forms of creative thinking, as people want to think of a reason for getting to use the cool machinery.

However, not all the initial reception to the program has been positive. There were a few people who initially questioned why the library would purchase an expensive 3-D printer and whether it was something that should be used in a library setting. But these complaints have been relatively few. Staff understand why the 3-D printer was purchased, and they use this understanding to defend its purchase when community members question it. For the most part, these community members have been satisfied with the answers they have received.

■ ■ ■

Like so many libraries, the staff at the makerspace has a running list of dream goals and ideas that they hope to someday implement at the library should the stars align. Some of the future goals for the makerspace are to get woodworking and metal-working kits and tools. They want teens to be exposed to as many possible methods of creation. The woodworking tools will hopefully be able to give their teens an immediate appreciation of what they have created, and likewise with the metal working. The benefits of having a makerspace allow for many such new ideas to be implemented in a learning space, with very few limitations. However, each of these ideas at Urbana Free Library will take much thought in terms of how to adequately protect teens for their safety while keeping it as a fun space to learn in a DIY fashion. At the moment they are currently exploring their options to see if acquiring these tools is a reasonable possibility.

Although the Urbana Free Library program is still in its infancy, teens have reacted well, in part because of the DIY approach and in part because it was a program well suited to their needs. The library wants to bring this makerspace program to their adult populations, and they have been working on ways to change the programming to reflect the needs and attentions of adult users, who bring different ideas to the project. They hope and anticipate that this will be a program

that sticks around for a long time to come.

VALDOSTA STATE UNIVERSITY, ODOM LIBRARY

Valdosta, GA
www.valdosta.edu/academics/library/
Academic Library

Based in South Georgia close to the Florida state line, Valdosta State University is a mid-sized public university that provides a liberal arts education to its 13,000+ FTE students with many students focused on humanities and education. They have created a makerspace for all students within their library that opened to the public in the fall 2013 semester, but at the time of this writing, some students had privately tested out the space.

CREATION

Michael Holt is a curious man. While listening to NPR's Science Friday one afternoon, he first heard about the concept of hackerspaces and makerspaces. Quickly he realized that this was something that he could bring into the library at Valdosta State. He began to assess what the library already had and brought the idea to his director, asking if it seemed feasible. When approval was given, he set about trying to establish a makerspace in the library through unused space in the library.

FUNDING

Due to the high cost of many of the materials required to set up a makerspace, libraries are often required to think outside the box when it comes to finding unique funding sources. This can be through grants, fundraisers, or many other special one-time funds for special purchases. The Odom Library was lucky to get special funding to purchase two of their Makerbot replicators from a University Academic Equipment Funding pool, which greatly eased potential costs.

Looking for such in-house grants can give libraries a greater shot at being accepted and receiving these grants, because there will be fewer applicants. Additionally, many of the people distributing these funds will have firsthand experience with your library and services, and will hopefully be aware of why there is a need for your request.

Fees

Continual funding can usually be built into a library's budget, but there are some items where a fee must be put in place. The Valdosta State Library has chosen not to charge their users for actual use of the space, but they do want to recoup their expenses on some of the projects that cost slightly more than others, such as the materials that will be used for 3-D printing or electoral circuit making. Right now the plan is to charge at cost rather than to try and turn a profit. As long as it is sustainable to only charge for materials fees, the library has no current plans to charge for the use of the room.

PHYSICAL SPACE

Located on the third floor of the library, Valdosta's makerspace is nestled among other study rooms. A rectangular space, the room is only 10 feet by 30 feet, yet manages to accommodate about ten patrons at peak capacity.

One of the primary benefits to using and taking advantage of this space was that it was already free and guaranteed. Projects can sometimes be derailed if there is not a space where they can take off and flourish. The Odom Library took advantage of having a free room available and didn't waste time on setting up shop. There was already a media center in the library where students could check out electronics, but the purpose of this makerspace was to help students with digital media projects. The library wanted to make a separate space from the media center to differentiate the makerspace. They did not want to check out materials to their students in this new space; they just wanted to create a space for their students to work collaboratively with some light instruction. In the media center there is little instruction offered to the students who check out materials.

Noise Issues

There was initial concern that, due to the small space, there might be too much noise pollution for the other nearby study rooms, as the room is equipped with a server rack and an AC unit that runs at all hours. But the reverse has proven true: the white noise created by these machines ends up cancelling out the noise from the study rooms. In fact, the portable AC unit had to be brought in due to the heat from all the machines running in such a small space.

TOOLS

Deciding how to equip a new makerspace is a daunting challenge for any library. After all, there can be an array of choices and technologies as well as the associated range of prices that can come with these technologies. Libraries deal with the competing issues of wanting the best and most innovative materials and needing to keep things under budget and in a state that they will not need to be replaced often beyond minimum maintenance. No piece of machinery lasts forever, but on the flip side of the coin, nobody wants to continually have to repurchase shoddy equipment. Networking with the campus IT people alerted maker staff to a previously unseen opportunity: good technology that had been surplused was made available.

Using this knowledge, the Valdosta State Library was able to purpose their makerspace with surplus IT equipment and to gather materials that would work for as many students and projects as possible. All this technology was perfectly good and serviceable, just items that had been replaced by newer models for various reasons. This equipment may not represent the latest available model, but the library has found that they do not need cutting-edge technology. They just need basics that they can use for their makerspace.

Even the furnishings in the space were found through surplus university furniture. It is a true example of looking through what you have and repurposing it to a different need. This in itself can be seen as a form of making by creating something new out of something old.

The staff at Valdosta took advantage of the resources they had available to them and ran with it. For libraries that are hesitating about creating a makerspace due to worries about finding space and funding for it, take a look at the types of spare furniture and rooms that are at your library or university. There may be a lot of resources that you just have not considered because you have gotten used to seeing them in your library. Repurposing old technology and furniture can help to create a space that already fits in with your library architecture and create a natural flow and feel.

The equipment at Valdosta runs a wide gamut, allowing for many different user types and programs. The library wanted their users to be able to experience a wide variety of technologies, since most students don't have access to all these technologies. They also figured that this learning lab could also help students later on as staff were trying to figure out if they wanted to purchase a particular model of machinery. Whether the purchasing process was a positive or a negative experience,

95

they wanted it to give them the opportunity to choose for themselves rather than basing the decision off of some other arbitrary factor.

Some of the machinery in the makerspace includes: two iMacs running OS 10.7, two HP desktops running Ubuntu Linux, as well as two Makerbot Replicators that only recently arrived. They already have a variety of ideas lined up for how to take advantage of the 3-D printers, but particularly they want to teach the students how to use programs like AutoCAD to create some of their own 3-D objects with the printers.

Because the printers are so new to the library, the library is currently exploring to see what type of options they have. It is all new to the librarians, and they want to learn just as much as their students do. Development kits for iOS and Android apps have been included on these computers so that students will have the option to try and develop their own apps, tapping into a market that is currently making a great splash among smartphone users and even web development. Many of these machines were chosen either because they could be gotten for free or at a very low comparative cost.

The Makerbots were the most expensive item, and were chosen over Solidoodle's 3-D printers primarily because they had the shortest delivery and build time in comparison to other 3-D printers that were on the market at the time of the creation of Valdosta's makerspace. The arrival of the Makerbots created a great splash on campus, and although the space had yet to be officially opened at the time of this writing, at least one or two students were frequently in the space creating a high demand for the 3-D printers.

The most interesting part of this is that news of the Makerbots arrival seems to have spread solely by word of mouth. There was no direct marketing put into their arrival, but already students were learning about it from one another, and thus the high demand is created for the space. Part of the reason that many of these machines were chosen was based not only availability, but based on expectations and anticipations of what students were most interested in.

STAFFING

Some libraries have chosen to have full-time staff members dedicated to running their space and planning the marketing and programming of the space, but not all libraries have the funds and resources for that to be a long-term project. In this case, Valdosta State has chosen not to staff the space, instead opting to allow students to "check out" the space as if it were just any other specialty study room. The purpose is twofold: it allows students to have private access to the materials, and it gives staff an easy way to keep statistics on how many people are using the space and at what peak times.

That said, the space is not entirely unsupervised. Regular staff at the university regularly swing by the space to double-check that all the machinery is running smoothly and to see if anyone using the space has any questions or unvoiced needs. Usually questions are resolved quickly, and most issues revolve around needing instruction in how to use machinery. (During the testing period, students used the space only on an as-needed basis. Once it opens fully in the fall 2013 semester, the space should really take off, and there will be better reporting of major issues.)

Another bonus to having minimal staff supervision is that it allows for the students to feel that this is really "their" space that they are getting to participate in and control how it functions and is used. After all, this space is really for the students; if they did not feel like it was their space, who would end up using it? By limiting staffing to simply checking in and observing from time to time, the staff at Valdosta have encouraged students to view the space in the best light possible.

PROGRAMMING

It is not enough to simply have a makerspace; plans must be made for how to program and market the space so that it does not go to waste. Each library makes its own decisions on this issue. Makerspaces are wonderful because they allow for a wide variety of technologies to be experienced and items to be created for users who typically would not have the option to use high-end equipment or want to spend hundreds (sometimes thousands!) of dollars for a project where they will only need the machine once.

The Odom Library at Valdosta State University has a wide variety of programming plans, such as: Introduction to Open Source/Linux, Introduction to Networking, Basic Computer Security, Lockpicking, Basic Electronic Circuit Working, and Metalworking, with the eventual goal to hold a makerfair each fall at the start of the new academic year. Their programming plan was to think of both short-term and long-term events that would get students to return to the space (and that hopefully would be slowly spread by word of mouth).

As with so many makerspaces, some of the first events that have taken place already involve very unique and creative items. One student has begun the process of creating an animated short using Blender, an open-source 3-D suite. Not all projects need be solo though. One group of students is in the midst of a long-term project to create a DIY book scanner for the library, with the eventual plan to turn the scanner into something that the library can use for its own projects down the line.

One of the things makerspaces have been greatly touted for is in encouraging young women to get involved in STEM fields (science, technology, engineering, and mathematics), and many people have been curious to know how this is specifically breaking down to get women into these fields. It is an encouraging sign to see that girls aren't afraid to enter these spaces and create.

Makerspaces are great advocates for the STEM fields in part because they encompass a great deal of the skills and knowledge needed for those fields, while simultaneously managing to make them approachable to the lay person. A great number of people are often dissuaded from entering these fields, because they mistakenly believe that they don't have the knowledge or capacity to fully understand them. Makerspaces succeed in making these fields approachable, while not stressing one particular field over the other. A project can take a bit of mathematics, a bit of science, and a bit of engineering to fully create. When users are allowed to see that they have the potential in them to create so much more than they had previously believed they unlock a great deal of belief in themselves as well as in others.

Gaming

Other planned events throughout the year include a Minecraft build challenge. For those unfamiliar with the game, Minecraft is a computer-based game where users literally move blocks around, break them, and place them. The object of the game is to build and destroy anything. One way to think of it is as a digital sandbox, where almost anything is possible. A build challenge involves having a group of people come together to build a common goal or object together or even sometimes to compete to see who can create the best or most unique object.

One of the unique things to the Valdosta State makerspace is that they have created a dedicated server just for Minecraft in the hopes to get people thinking about the unique ways of creating something that is not necessarily a physical item that can be held in one's hand. Many libraries are looking for ways to incorporate other types of gaming into their makerspaces. The Odom Library wanted to put its focus on Minecraft because they felt it would offer their students a chance to create structures that they would not normally have the option to create, all while giving them an opportunity to work together and get to know their fellow students.

Another event in the making is an InfoSec Capture the Flag Tournament. InfoSec is short for *information security*; during the event, teams compete to test their knowledge and skills in various areas of digital security. Prior to the event, students will be taught the basics of information security, which can involve everything from web security to reverse engineering and network analysis.

Events similar to these things have been held formally and informally by other universities and communities across the country, though rarely targeted solely at undergraduate students. The technology is important, but to the people who run the makerspace, the most important part of providing access to these technologies is in making sure that the students who use the space learn not only how to use the techonologies, but the safe and smart ways to take advantage of it. Each of these events has been planned to take place at key points during the semester when students are most likely to attend or need a break, such as during midterms and finals week.

99

MARKETING

The programming and the creation of a space is not enough to bring people there. If people do not know it exists, how can they use it? The people at Valdosta have laid out a multitiered marketing strategy to make students more aware of the space, and most important, more likely to use it. Again, social media is playing a huge role in getting the word out. An important part of marketing is in targeting who sees your advertisements and making sure that the right people see them when they need to see them. By taking advantage of social media, the library is planning on getting students where they suspect that they spend most of their time: online.

Blog entries and Facebook posts are the two major ways that they are planning on attacking the social media front, encouraging people to like the new makerspace and advertising special events through it. They have over six hundred likes. These likes are people who see the library's updates and who can be influenced to come to their makerspace based on the posts that they add to their Facebook pages.

The library also has several digital signs that they use to display posters and signs that scroll by for students to see as they enter the building. These are displayed on large monitors throughout the library so that they can display bright and attention-catching slides to students and other passersby.

In addition to making students more aware on the digital front, several events are planned for the beginning of the year that will do more to demonstrate to students what the space is capable of. For example, the library is in the middle of creating its own mini makerfair for students as a semester kickoff event.

STAFFING

A library makerspace cannot exist alone. There must be people there to help facilitate and run the space so that things go smoothly. The space needs little supervision, but Michael Holt helps monitor what the space needs and bring in whatever is needed at the time. Between him and few student workers, they can go upstairs and monitor use of the space from time to time, without overburdening their schedules.

One of the personal goals Holt had was to show that libraries do not need to have expensive budgets to get a makerspace off the ground. Using creative thinking and networking with people who were able to help him get the ball rolling, Holt kept the total cost for the space under $6,000. Money is often cited as one of the biggest impediments for libraries to get projects started and funded, but the Odom Library proves that a massive budget is not required to create a makerspace. It simply relies on the ingenuity and creativity of the people willing to make it work.

DEMOGRAPHICS

Located less than twenty miles from the border of Florida along the I-75 corridor, The Odom Library is an academic library in South Georgia. The core of their collection is focused on undergraduate studies, particularly in education, as the school was started in 1906 as a state normal college for women.

Valdosta students who have done the initial trial runs for the makerspace have grasped the concept and need for a makerspace immediately. It is hard for the library to tell when the peak times will be as of yet, since as of this writing the space has not been fully opened up to the public. They have had special events for classes and trainings, and during those times they have had high attendance. They anticipate that once the space has completely opened up and received a high amount of marketing, use of the space will go up greatly. So far the students using the space have predominately been male, although the presence of female students is not unheard of there.

Holt and his colleague Ed Braun were proven right in their idea that a collaborative learning space for majors beyond just computer science majors was needed. The types of majors that have been using the space have been all over the map, with everything from art majors to history majors. Oftentimes people can have a limited view when thinking of how these spaces can be used, but the most important part to stress is that makerspaces are for everybody. They should not be limited to just one particular type of student or user. They need to be made available to all, in part, because there is power in learning together. Everyone brings their own unique set of information tools to the discussion, and if everyone is working together from the same vantage point they might completely overlook what another person sees as obvious.

Forms

At the present the library does not have any liability waivers in place, but discussion whether one is truly needed is under way.

■ ■ ■

Valdosta State's library is taking an emphasis on transforming what they have available to them (unused rooms) and turning it into valuable space that students want to actually use. It is a continually evolving space, similar to many makerspaces highlighted in this book. The library will take what works and throw away that which does not, while remaining open to the possibility of new things to try.

Makerspaces give the freedom to experiment and see what does and does not work. When I first started researching the Valdosta State makerspace, it was still in its nascent stage. Over the process of writing this book, I have gotten the chance to see their space change and evolve from its early days to its current form, which is much more focused and changed from its beginnings. I have no doubt that when I next check up on them after the publication of this book that they will be doing something else new and unique. Such is the power of makerspaces. They are not duty bound to carry out the same plans and measures that they have been doing for so long.

The key components for transforming these rooms into a makerspace involved faculty and staff collaboration, as well as unused materials—both in physical space and in terms of computers that could be repurposed. Although the makerspace occupies a small area, staff have made it into a fully functional space that students are excited to come into and explore their creativity within.

Conclusion

Makerspaces take many forms, each with different missions and target populations. What they all share is the spirit of innovation and an enthusiasm to turn their patrons from passive receivers of information into active creators who have a small part in understanding the world around them.

Since I first began working on this project in 2012, makerspaces have blossomed in the media. Some people argue that they are just the latest library fad; others remain cautious about 3-D printers because of potential abuses, such as the controversies at the time of this writing surrounding the Liberator, the world's first 3-D-printed gun. These are all valid concerns for a library that wants to make sure that it only does the best for its patrons. Perhaps I am biased, but I do not believe the makerspace movement is a true fad that will fade away in the next few years. In fact, many are predicting that 3-D printing in particular will get much cheaper as key patents begin to expire. Certainly, many people seem to be putting their hopes into makerspaces and 3-D printing. Just walking through the exhibition floor of the ALA conference, one can see a shift in what the major companies are pushing to libraries, with many trying to sell 3-D printers and displaying the types of objects that can be made.

Similarly, I do not believe that 3-D printers are a great danger to our libraries. Libraries like SUNY Oswego have put in place rules to stop their patrons from creating materials that would lead to guns, and it certainly would not be out of line for other libraries worried about such things to create their own similar policies.

Libraries will always be needed in the world, but the services they provide are bound to shift as the culture shifts. Very few libraries still use a card catalog; most have slowly shifted over to OPACs. While it's doubtful that all libraries will eventually transition into having makerspaces, I believe it will be common in the future to see dedicated spaces for patrons to work with librarians toward thinking creatively and developing life skills. I firmly believe that makerspaces are the current iteration of meeting patron needs. Libraries and librarians have to be practical by nature, and if the makerspace were not a needed thing in a library, we simply would not be expending the great amounts of money, time, and space into turning sections of our libraries into makerspaces. Certainly the term is something on a lot of lips right now, giving it the air of a fad, but the spaces will stay. These are things that libraries have made a commitment to supporting over the next several years.

If you or your library is trying to decide whether or not to create a makerspace in your library, ask yourself the following questions:

- Why do we need a makerspace?
- Can we afford it?
- Do we have the physical space for it?
- How will we program for it?
- What type of equipment do we need to support it?
- Do we have the staff and time to provide support for new equipment?

If your library is able to plan a strategy based around these questions, then it might be something worth considering. Certainly the highlighted libraries in this book have shown examples to build from and to create your own ideas for making your own unique makerspace.

REFERENCE

Mims, Christopher. 2013. "3D Printing Will Explode in 2014, Thanks to the Expiration of Key Patents." Quartz, July 21. Accessed August 9, 2013. http://qz.com/106483/3-D-printing-will-explode-in-2014-thanks-to-the-expiration-of-key-patents/.

Resources

Featured Libraries

Anchorage Public Library
3600 Denali Street
Anchorage, AK 99503
(907) 343-2975
www.muni.org/DEPARTMENTS/
   LIBRARY/PAGES/DEFAULT.ASPX

Brooklyn Public Library
280 Cadman Plaza W
Brooklyn, NY 11201
(718) 623-7100
www.bklynpubliclibrary.org

Carnegie Public Library
4400 Forbes Avenue
Pittsburgh, PA 15213
(412) 622-3114
www.clpgh.org

Cleveland Public Library
325 Superior Ave E
Cleveland, OH
(216) 623-2800
www.cpl.org

Georgia Tech Library
704 Cherry St
Atlanta, GA 30332
(404) 894-4500
www.library.gatech.edu

Mesa Public Library–Red Mountain Branch
635 N Power Rd
Mesa, AZ 85205
(480) 644-3183
www.mesalibrary.org

Michigan Makers
East Middle School
1042 S Mill St
Plymouth, MI 48170
(734) 416-4950
http://michiganmakers.weebly.com/

Urbana Free Library
210 W Green St
Urbana, IL 61801
(217) 367-4057
http://urbanafreelibrary.org/

Valdosta State University–Odom Library
1500 Patterson Street
Valdosta, GA 31698
(229) 333-5869
www.valdosta.edu/academics/library/

Featured Resources

Arduino Boards
www.arduino.cc
A small single-board microcontroller for coding a variety of projects.

K'Nex Toys
www.knex.com
Children's construction blocks and toys often used to create complex designs.

Makerbots
www.makerbot.com
One of the major producers of 3-D printers.

Solidoodle
www.solidoodle.com
Alternative 3-D printers that many libraries have adopted.

Thingiverse
www.thingiverse.com
Maintained by Makerbot, the site is a great resource for 3-D files and project ideas.

Makerspaces for Libraries Survey

My initial work on this book began with distributing this survey across several major library listservs and asking anyone for responses from libraries who currently had a makerspace or had plans to create one in the near future. I received many responses from libraries and librarians across the nation who were just beginning their initial process of creation. The libraries included in this book all filled out the following survey; afterward I contacted each of them and began to interview them more in depth. I include the survey below so that others may get an idea of how the research was conducted.

■ ■ ■

This survey is intended for libraries that either already have a makerspace in use OR those that are currently in the process of creating one. If you have not yet implemented your makerspace yet, please answer the questions as you best anticipate the response to be.

Part One—Physical Space

1. Describe your physical aspects of your makerspace: What are the dimensions? Where is it in the library?
2. Are there noise issues with the space?
3. How many people may use the space at one time?
4. What type of materials did you need to create the space?
5. Did you have space ready for the makerspace or did you repurpose an already existing space?
6. What are the core machines and devices used in your makerspace?

7. Why did you choose one type of device over another?

8. How do you staff the makerspace?

Part Two—Programming & Marketing

1. How have you alerted patrons to the creation and availability of the makerspace?

2. What type of programs do you have for the makerspace?

3. What population are these programs aimed at?

4. How frequently is the makerspace in use?

5. Do you have a unique project that you always have users make in the makerspace or does it vary?

6. How does this differ from a typical library work room for things like knitting club and story time?

7. Have you created release forms or other type of permission forms for users to use the makerspace?

8. Do you have any interesting statistics about the makerspace use that you would like to share?

Part Three—Demographics

1. What type of library do you work in?

2. Describe your user base: What is your typical patron like?

3. How receptive were your users to the makerspace? Did they initially understand the idea?

4. When are the peak times for use of the makerspace? Morning? Afternoon? Weekends?

5. What part of the country is your library based in?

6. Did you receive any grants or other special financial support to create your makerspace?

7. How did your library conceive of the idea for a makerspace?

8. Do patrons have to pay a fee to use or create materials in the makerspace?

Index

CPSIA information can be obtained at www.ICGtesting.com
Printed in the USA
LVOW12s1455090514

385159LV00019B/1335/P

9 781555 709907